SEWING FOR A
Royal Baby

22 HEIRLOOM PATTERNS
for your little prince or princess

EDITORS OF
Sew Beautiful
MAGAZINE

Sew Beautiful

EDITORS
Amelia Johanson, Kathy Barnard

DESIGNERS
Julia Boyles, Leighann Lott

LAYOUT
Courtney Kyle

ILLUSTRATIONS
Angela Atherton, Wendy Schoen,
Kathy Barnard, Sue Friend

PHOTOGRAPHY
Jennifer & Company, Mac Jamieson (pages 34, 35,
and 41)

PRODUCTION
Katherine Jackson

Sew Beautiful

Manufactured in the United States
by RR Donnelley Roanoke

Library of Congress CIP data not available
at time of printing

ISBN 978-1-878048-81-3 (pbk.)
ISBN 978-1-878048-83-7 (PDF)

10 9 8 7 6 5 4 3 2 1

Dedication

This book is dedicated to Martha Campbell Pullen for the love
and support she has given to everyone in her extended sewing
family, and for sharing her beliefs, her business and her passion
for heirloom sewing with the world.

Contents

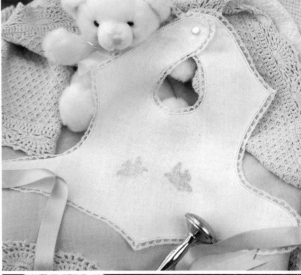

*L*IKE THE REST OF THE WORLD, we at *Sew Beautiful* are delighted whenever we hear news that a new little prince or princess will be welcomed into England's Royal Family. Of course our thoughts go immediately to the most famous royal christening gown, which was originally commissioned in 1841 by Queen Victoria for her first child. The gown of Spitalfield silk satin and Honiton lace was worn by centuries of royal babies including Prince Charles and Prince William. No longer in wearable condition, it was retired by Queen Elizabeth who commissioned a replica of the gown to be worn for the 2008 christening of her grandson Viscount Sever. Will new royals continue to be baptized in this royal christening robe, carrying the tradition into the next century? Or will something new be designed for the heir to the Throne of England?

After looking at various historical photos of the family gown, we simply couldn't resist coming up with our own version. After all, remaking vintage baby clothing is our specialty. One photo led to another—little Prince William in his smocked suits, Princess Margaret in an adorable organdy dress—and it reminded us that the world is forever fascinated by what the royal family wears. Kate Middleton's Alexander McQueen (by Sarah Burton) wedding gown set the standard for the entire bridal industry; why shouldn't our little ones have a standard of their own? In this book, we present *Sew Beautiful's* vision of what finery for babies and toddlers should be. Some pieces have been inspired by actual royal children's attire, some we first saw at the Victoria & Albert Museum of Childhood in the Bethnal Green area of London, some are remakes of antiques purchased along Portobello Road and yet others are favorites we pulled from previous issues of *Sew Beautiful* magazine. Patterns for every look in this book are included on the CD-rom. We've included a variety of different embellishment techniques that set clothes you create for your children apart from anything you can buy. The size ranges vary from a single infant size, to 1 to 6 depending on the pattern. Most of the embroidery designs (hand or machine) and appliqué designs are included on the CD-rom. Classic techniques common to children's apparel and heirloom sewing, as well as handwork diagrams, can be referenced in the Techniques section on page 124. As with any *Sew Beautiful* pattern, we've listed the materials we used to create our vision so you can duplicate what you see here. But we also encourage you to choose your own fabrics and trims to create a wardrobe that suits your little prince or princess to a royal T.

Sew on, sew well, Sew Beautiful,

The editors of *Sew Beautiful* Magazine

SEWING FOR A

Christening

ACHRISTENING OR BAPTISM IS THE FIRST OCCASION in a child's life
that is steeped in faith and sentiment. The traditional mode of dress, the long,
elaborate gown, often a family heirloom worn for generations, was sanctioned
in Victorian times. Gowns, then, were required by the church to be white, a
symbol of purity and the cleansing of sin. Over time, this mandate relaxed, and
christening gowns, like wedding gowns, now reflect the tastes of the family.
Probably the most famous gown was commissioned in 1941 by Queen Victoria
and was subsequently worn by most members of the royal family. It's only fitting
that when the gown deteriorated beyond a wearable state, Queen Elizabeth
commissioned a replica, presumably to carry on the royal tradition. Our version of
this royal gown is machine embroidered with elegant motifs. Where pleated silk
ribbons serpentine down the original skirt, we've used gathered strips of netting,
or you could follow the path with softly shaped lace insertion. Our boy's design
is a tailored treasure made in a pale blue batiste, fashioned prior to construction
into meticulous folds of fabric. The longer sleeve speaks to more tepid climates,
or you could shorten the sleeve pattern for a warm-weather christening. Whether
your special occasion is for a little prince or princess, the memories begin with
the first stitch and endure for generations.

Royal Netting Christening Gown

CONSTRUCTED BY CONNIE PALMER, DIRECTIONS BY KATHY BARNARD

December 15, 1948, at Buckingham Palace, London, Princess Elizabeth holds the month-old royal prince. Seated to the left is Queen Elizabeth, the infant's grandmother. Standing in the rear is the prince's father, the Duke of Edinburgh. The child was christened Prince Charles Philip Arthur George of Edinburgh. (AP Photo)

GENERATIONS OF BRITISH ROYAL BABIES, from Princess Victoria in 1841 to Princess Eugenie in 1990, were christened in the elaborate royal gown of Spitalfield silk satin and Honiton lace commissioned by Queen Victoria. Having finally deteriorated beyond a wearable state, the gown was retired five years ago and replaced by a replica commissioned by Queen Elizabeth. Although photographs of the exquisite gown exist, the details aren't readily apparent. What can be discerned is the magnificent pleated ribbon design on the skirt that serpentines around circular embroidery motifs. We made that the focus of our Royal Netting Christening Gown, choosing a Zundt motif you can purchase as a download. Instead of pleating yards of ribbon, which would have weighed heavily on the diaphanous netting, Connie Palmer used a ruched netting technique to achieve a similar effect. Both the overdress and the slip are edged in a gathered 7" (18 cm) wide netting lace, which also serves as the exquisite portrait collar. True to the original, we added the finishing touch of silk satin sashing tied in an off-center bow at the neckline.

What You'll Need...

PATTERN
(available on the CD-rom)

"Royal Netting Christening Gown" (sizes 6 to 9 mos.)

Overdress

    Front high yoke

    Back high yoke

    Puffed sleeve

    Front over dress curve template

    Underarm curve template

Overdress front and back skirts (no pattern required)

Slip Pattern

    Front bodice

    Back bodice

Slip front and back skirts (no pattern required)

FABRIC
(layout guide provided on the CD-rom)

5 yd (4.6 m) of ivory heirloom cotton netting for the overdress (15 percent shrinkage is calculated in the yardage requirement)

2 yd (1.8 m) of ivory heirloom cotton netting for the netting ruffle strips

2½ yd (2¼ m) of ivory satin batiste for the slip

½ yd (45.5 cm) of ivory silk organza for the yoke interlining

LACE

14 yd (12.8 m) of 7" (18 cm) wide English netting lace from Capitol Imports for the overdress, collar and slip

¾ yd (68.5 cm) of 1" (2.5 cm) wide lace edging for the slip and overdress plackets

NOTIONS

Three ⅜" (1 cm) mother-of-pearl buttons for slip back closure

Three ⅜" (1 cm) mother-of-pearl buttons for overdress closure (optional); may use beauty pins

2 yd (1.8 m) of 2" (5 cm) wide silk satin ribbon (optional for neck embellishment)

SUPPLIES

50 wt Mettler thread for construction (color Blanc)

Six small spools of Madeira 50 wt cotton for machine embroidery (accommodates top and bobbin threading)

Twelve pre-wound bobbins (white)

Universal size 80 machine needles for construction

Machine embroidery needles for embroidery

Floriani Wet N Gone stabilizer (non-tacky) or any non-tacky water-soluble stabilizer. NOTE: *Sticky stabilizers are too tacky for netting.*

Sulky KK 2000 temporary spray adhesive

Machine gathering foot. NOTE: *This is not optional for this volume of gathering.*

Blue wash-away marking pen

Glass head pins

Cutting mat and rotary cutter

Clear quilting ruler

Spray starch

EMBROIDERY DESIGNS
(must be purchased separately)

Circle is from Zundt Designs— Flower 28-1 (design #202135-1) (Single download can be purchased from *www.zundtdesign.com.*)

Scallop below circle (flower and vine) is from the *Martha Pullen Vintage Collection Vol 1, Disk 2* (design #MPC 06024 and MPC 06022) from store.marthapullen.com.

What to Cut...

FROM STARCHED NETTING

One yoke front

Two yoke backs

Two sleeves

Three skirt blocks 46" (117 cm) long across width of netting (this creates two fronts and one back)

Two sleeve binding strips on the bias 2" × 9" (5 × 23 cm)

One binding strip for neck on the bias 2" × 12½" (5 × 31.5 cm)

FROM NON-STARCHED NETTING

Ruffle strips 1" (2.5 cm) wide × width of fabric (see cutting instructions on page 11)

FROM SILK ORGANZA

One yoke front for interlining

Two yoke backs for interlining

Two sleeve binding strips on the bias 2" × 9" (5 × 23 cm) (binding interlining)

One binding strip for neck on the bias 2" × 12½" (5 × 31.5 cm) (binding interlining)

FROM SATIN BATISTE

One slip front bodice

Two slip back bodices

Two skirt blocks (39" [99 cm] long × width of fabric) (creates a front and a back skirt) NOTE: *The length of the slip with a lace hem finishes to the exact length of the overdress. If you wish for the lace hem of the slip to hang below the lace hem of the overdress, add 3"–5" (7.5–12.5 cm) to the slip skirt length.*

How to Make It...

Preparation...

1 Wash the netting fabric, batiste, organza and all the lace before cutting or embroidering. Soak in warm water, squeeze out the excess water in a towel; air dry.

2 Reserve 2 yd (1.8 m) of netting for the ruffles and press without starch. Press the remaining netting, batiste and lace with light starch. (Netting shrinks to about 36" [91.5 cm] wide.)

Cutting Ruffle Strips the Easy Way

You will need about forty-six 1" (2.5 cm) wide strips cut 36" (91.5 cm) long to create 23 yd (21 m) of gathered ruffles for the overdress and slip.

1 Roll up the 2 yd (1.8 m) of pressed but unstarched netting like a jellyroll or fold it on itself lengthwise until you have folded it into a narrow, layered stack (around 4"–6" [10–15 cm] wide or so).

2 Place the roll or stack on a cutting mat. Place a clear quilting ruler on top of the netting and slice off the end of the stack to even it up with a clean cut. Discard the end (**FIG. 1**).

3 Mark and cut 1" (2.5 cm) wide strips from the roll. Make sure that

you do not cut them at an angle, or you will have oddly shaped strips. Keep the edge of the ruler even with the fold edge of the roll. Each cut unrolls to reveal a perfect netting strip. Use the remaining yardage to cut the bias neck and sleeve binding strips (see layout on CD-rom).

Marking
Front Skirt

(Refer to skirt **FIGS. 2 and 3** for marking.) Circles are represented on the figure to show the spacing. You do not have to draw circles on your fabric; only center dots or cross marks.

1 Pin the netting block onto a large cardboard grid of blocking board. If you do not have a board, pin to the tissue paper marked with horizontal and vertical lines. This helps you keep it square and stable while you mark.

2 Mark a line 6" (15 cm) from the bottom edge and another line 6" (15 cm) from the center front edge (line A shown in blue).

3 Mark the next lines 3" (7.5 cm) from the 6" (15 cm) lines (line B shown in red).

4 The first circle to mark will be the third circle from the side edge. It is

from this circle that all the others are marked. Mark a dot or crosshair on the horizontal line A 11" (28 cm) from the vertical line A (**FIG. 3**).

5 From this dot, mark two more dots 6" (15 cm) apart on the horizontal line A for the next two circles at the hem.

6 There are two circles placed at an angle that create the curved front corner of the overdress. To mark the center of the first corner circle, measure over 6" (15 cm) from the first hemline circle center and 1¼" (3.2 cm) from the horizontal line A (**FIG. 3**).

7 Mark the next corner circle 6¼" (16 cm) from the horizontal line A and 1¼" (3.2 cm) from the vertical line A (**FIG. 3**).

8 There are four more circles placed along the vertical line A all spaced 6" (15 cm) on the center from the corner angled circle (**FIGS. 1 AND 2**).

9 The flower/vine scallop design is set below every other circle starting with the top circle motif on vertical line A. Extend the centerlines from the circle to meet line B (this will mark the center of the scallop design) (see red semicircle marks on **FIGS. 2 AND 3**).

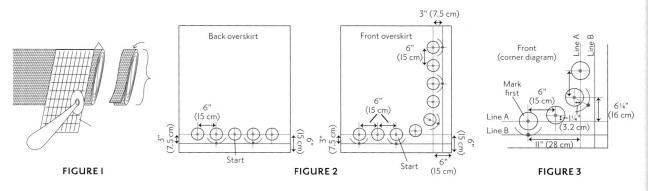

FIGURE 1

FIGURE 2

FIGURE 3

Back Skirt

(refer to **FIG. 2** for marking)

1 Pin the netting to stabilize it while marking it in the same manner as suggested for the front blocks (Step I above).

2 Mark line A 6" (15 cm) from the bottom edge of the back block (shown in blue).

3 Mark line B 3" (7.5 cm) below line A (shown in red).

4 Mark the center circle first on line A at the center of the back block. Mark the next circle centers spaced 6" (15 cm) apart (two to the left of center and two to the right of center for a total of five circles).

5 Mark the flower/vine scallop motifs under each circle to the left and right of the center as shown in red on line B in **FIG. 3**.

NOTE: *There are five circles embroidered over the side seams after they are stitched. Instructions for marking will be included in the embroidery instructions that follow.*

Embroidery

1 Embroider all the circle motifs first. Hoop Wet N Gone stabilizer; mark the centers while in the hoop. Spray the stabilizer with KK 2000 (never spray the fabric). Place the netting to the stabilizer aligning the vertical and horizontal centers of the fabric to the center marked on the stabilizer. Cut another piece of Wet N Gone stabilizer to place on top of the netting. Spray the stabilizer piece with KK 2000 and fuse over the top of the netting making a stabilizer/netting sandwich.

2 Stitch out the motif with Blanc 50 wt Mettler thread in the needle and a pre-wound bobbin in the bobbin case.

3 Cut away the excess stabilizer to neaten the area and continue to the next circle. Repeat the process until all the circles on each netting block are complete.

4 Repeat the hooping process to stitch out each of the flower/vine scallop designs below each designated circle.

5 Mark the side seam stitching lines ¾" (2 cm) from the side circle motif so that the circle motif edges will sit 1½" (3.8 cm) apart (or 6" [15 cm] on center) once the seam is sewn. Mark this line all the way to the top of the skirt on each side of the back block and one side of each front block **(FIG. 4)**. Do not cut the seam allowance.

6 Align the stitching line and pin the seam. Stitch on the marked line. Stitch again ⅛" (3 mm) from the seam, stitching within the seam allowance. Trim off the seam allowance next to the second row of stitching and roll and whip the seam with a zigzag stitch.

7 Mark the centers for five circle motifs to be stitched over the seams. Set the first circle 6" (15 cm) from the circle centers at the bottom along the hem. Space each circle motif 6" (15 cm) apart on the center working from the bottom to the top **(FIG. 5)**.

8 Once the embroidery is complete, soak all three blocks in warm water overnight to remove the stabilizer and markings.

9 Remove the excess water by rolling the wet blocks in a towel. Allow to air dry. Press with light starch.

10 Mark a cutting line ¾" (2 cm) from the outer flower/vine scallops and use the curve template provided with the pattern on the CD-rom to mark and cut out the front pieces. Cut the bottom back ¾" (2 cm) from the scallop motifs **(SEE FIG. 5)**.

11 Divide the skirt into quarters and center the armhole curves on the front quarter marks using the template provided on the CD-rom **(SEE FIG. 5)**.

12 Stay-stitch on the arm curve seamlines and then cut out.

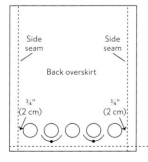
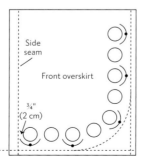

FIGURE 4

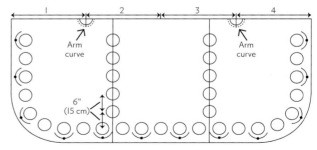

FIGURE 5

Netting Ruffles and Lace

Prepare Ruffles

1 Set up your machine with a gathering foot and 50 wt thread; select a straight stitch (L=2.5). NOTE: *This stitch length will automatically gather the strips.*

2 Center strips under the foot and gather each one; there is no need to connect the strips (keep them separated for easy application). When sewing onto the skirt, just overlap the ends a bit. After gathering, just leave them in a pile. They are easily untangled as you go because your strips are small (about 16" [40.5 cm] long).

Apply Ruffles

1 There is really no need to mark the serpentine design around the embroidery on the netting, as it is easy to "eye" an even placement as you go, and you want to avoid soaking to remove the marks once the ruffles are set. If you feel more comfortable with a guide, use an air-erasable marking pen.

2 Pin the first ruffle strip in place onto the netting skirt, starting at the top center front, working around the circle motif in and out so that the flower/vine scallop motifs are open (not covered by ruffles) (**FIG. 6**).

3 Place two to three strips, then stitch. You don't want to place them all and then try to navigate at the machine with all of those pins in your fabric. Stitch along the center over the gathering stitches using a lightning stitch on your machine. This stitch offers a slight amount of "give" to the stitching so that the stitches will not "snap" if the fabric is pulled or stretched later. Use a wooden skewer to help you direct and guide the ruffles under the foot as you sew.

4 Work the ruffles all around the outer circles and around the circles at each seam.

Prepare Lace Edging

1 Measure and cut a 4.8 yd (4.4 m) piece of English netting lace for the gathered edging.

2 Taper each end so that the lace will narrow as it reaches the top center. Mark over 2" (5 cm) from the embroidered edge at the end of the lace, and then mark down 25" (63.5 cm) along the raw edge of the lace. Use a ruler or straight edge to mark a tapered cutting line (**FIG. 7**). Cut the taper. Repeat on the other end of the strip.

3 Gather the lace using the gathering foot in the same manner as you stitched the netting ruffles. Stitch ½" (1.3 cm) from the edge (you may want to trim off the wavy raw edge of your lace if your lace has one).

4 Place the gathered edge of the lace to the edge of the embroidered netting skirt with the right sides together and the raw edges even. Straight-stitch with a ½" (1.3 cm) seam allowance. Stitch again ⅛" (3 mm) from the first stitching line within the seam allowance. Trim the seam next to the second line of stitching. Roll and whip the seam with a zigzag (**FIG. 8**).

5 Press the lace away from the skirt and the seam toward the skirt.

6 Cover the lace seam with the netting ruffle strips on the right side of the gown using a lightning stitch as before. Set the skirt aside to prepare the yoke and sleeves.

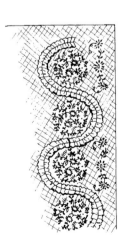

FIGURE 6

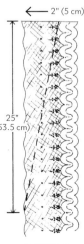

← 2" (5 cm)

25" (63.5 cm)

FIGURE 7

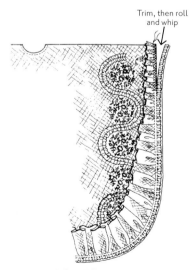

Trim, then roll and whip

FIGURE 8

Construction

Seam allowances are ½" (1.3 cm) unless otherwise noted.

Yoke

1 Place silk organza behind the netting on the front yoke; baste stitch ⅜" (1 cm) from the edge all around (**FIG. 9**).

2 Before basting the back yoke interlinings in place, stitch the back edge with a ¼" (6 mm) seam allowance (**FIG. 10**). Trim to ⅛" (3 mm) and then turn and press. Pin together the remaining edges and baste stitch. Press the back facing along the foldline indicated on the pattern.

3 Sew the front yoke to the back yoke at the shoulder seams with a French seam.

4 Cut a 38" (96.5 cm) piece of English netting lace for the collar

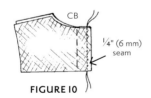

FIGURE 9

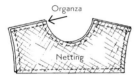

FIGURE 10

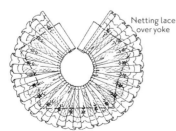

FIGURE 11

FIGURE 12

and trim the raw edge of the lace straight (cut away the wavy edge if it has one). Fold each raw end under ¼" (6 mm) twice and hem to finish the ends.

5 Run two rows of gathering stitches ⅜" (1 cm) and ⅝" (1.5 cm) from the raw edge. Pull the bobbin threads to gather the collar. Fit to the neck edge of the yoke. Place the hemmed ends ½" (1.3 cm) from each folded edge of the back yoke. Stitch in place with a ½" (1.3 cm) seam allowance (**FIG. 11**). Remove the gathering stitches beyond the seam.

6 Prepare the neck binding strip by placing the 2" (5 cm) bias strip of silk organza to the 2" (5 cm) bias strip of netting and sew a straight stitch down the center lengthwise. Press the strip in half along the stitching line (**FIG. 12**). Press the strip in a circle with the fold on the

FIGURE 13

FIGURE 14

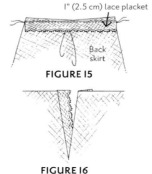

FIGURE 15

FIGURE 16

outer edge of the circle. Steam to shape the neck binding.

7 Pin the binding to the neck edge over the lace collar with the raw edges even. Allow ½" (1.3 cm) to extend on each end at the back yoke edges. Stitch a ½" (1.3 cm) seam. Stitch another row of stitching a scant ¼" (6 mm) from the seam. Trim the seam to a perfect and even ¼" (6 mm) width. Wrap the bias over the seam and place the fold edge of the bias to the wrong side of the yoke (**FIG. 13**). Hand whip the bias edge to the organza layer only. Fold under and tuck in the back ends of the binding to finish the back edges neatly. Set the yoke and collar aside to prepare the sleeves.

Sleeves

1 Stitch two rows of gathering stitches in the bottom edge and along the cap edge between the notches ⅜" (1 cm) and ⅝" (1.5 cm) from the raw edges.

2 Prepare the binding strip in the same manner as the neck binding with the silk organza interfacing.

3 Gather the bottom edge of the sleeve to fit the band, leaving 2" (5 cm) on each side flat and ungathered. Stitch a ½" (1.3 cm) seam (**FIG. 14**). Stitch again a scant ¼" (6 mm) from the seam stitching and trim just next to the stitching for a perfect and even ¼" (6 mm) seam allowance.

4 Wrap the binding around the seam and hand-stitch the fold edge to the stitching line on the wrong side of the sleeve in the same manner as the neck binding.

5 Sew the sleeve seam with a ½" (1.3 cm) seam allowance. Stitch again ⅛" (3 mm) from the seam stitching. Trim to the stitching and roll and whip the seam with a zigzag to finish. Set the sleeve aside for dress assembly.

Dress Assembly

1 Set a lace placket or an organza placket in the center back of the skirt (follow the placket instructions in the Techniques section starting on page 124). If using 1" (2.5 cm) lace edging for the placket, straight-stitch along the header edge of the lace along the stitching line of the skirt slit (catching the point at the center) **(FIG. 15)**. Then, roll and whip the seam with a zigzag. Press lace placket to the inside and treat in the same manner as a normal fabric placket **(FIG. 16)**.

2 Gather the top edges of the skirt in the front and backs with two rows of gathering stitches at $\frac{3}{8}$" (1 cm) and $\frac{5}{8}$" (1.5 cm).

3 Gather the front skirt to fit the front yoke bottom edge (flip the collar out of the way). Stitch a $\frac{1}{2}$" (1.3 cm) seam. Stitch again $\frac{1}{8}$" (3 mm) from the seam stitching. Trim to the stitching and roll and whip the seam with a zigzag to finish. You may also serge the edges with a 4-thread overlock stitch if you have a serger.

4 Gather the back skirt to each back yoke bottom edge. Unfold the facings of the yoke at the bottom edge and allow the left skirt placket to extend with the edge of the placket aligned to the foldline of the yoke facing. On the other side, fold the placket to the wrong side of the skirt and align the fold edge of the placket to the foldline of the right back yoke facing. Once sewn, fold back the facings to the inside of the dress and hand whip the bottom edge over the seam. The right back yoke will overlap the left back yoke.

5 Gather the sleeve caps and insert the sleeve into the armholes with the right sides together. Pull the lace collar out of the way. Stitch a $\frac{1}{2}$" (1.3 cm) seam. Stitch again $\frac{1}{8}$" (3 mm) from the seam stitching.

Trim to the stitching and roll and whip the seam with a zigzag to finish.

6 Stitch three buttonholes in the right side of the back yoke edge and three buttons on the left side. Or, you may opt to use beauty pins instead (available from *store.marthapullen.com*).

7 Tie a bow in the 2 yd (1.8 m) piece of ribbon. Trim the ends at an angle. Hand-tack the bow to the neck edge as desired.

Slip Instructions

1 Sew the front bodice to the back at the shoulder seams with a French seam.

2 Fold back the facing edges to the wrong side on the foldline and press. If back edge was not cut on the selvage, serge or zigzag to finish back raw edge.

3 For a scalloped finish on the edge of the neck and armholes, first sew a serger finish along the raw edge of the neck with the back facings still folded to the inside. Press the serged edge to the wrong side. Select an heirloom appliqué stitch (looks like $\_\_\_||\_\_\_$). This will make a pretty scalloped edge. Set the width at 5.0 and stitch with the straight stitches in the fabric and the zigzag stitches off the folded edge.

4 Sew the bodice side seams with a French seam. Set the bodice aside to prepare the skirt.

5 Sew one side seam of the skirt with a French seam, leaving the other open.

6 Sew the remaining English netting lace to the bottom edge of the slip with a $\frac{1}{2}$" (1.3 cm) seam. Stitch again $\frac{1}{8}$" (3 mm) from the seam stitching. Trim to the stitching and roll and whip the seam with

a zigzag to finish. Press the lace down and the seam up.

7 Stitch the remaining side seam with a French seam.

8 Cover the lace seam with netting ruffles.

9 Sew a placket in the center back skirt in the same manner as the netting skirt using lace, or use fabric and follow the placket instructions provided in the Techniques section on page 124.

10 Run two rows of gathering stitches in the front and back skirt top edges $\frac{3}{8}$" (1 cm) and $\frac{5}{8}$" (1.5 cm) from the raw edge.

11 Gather the skirt to fit the bottom edge of the bodice. At the center back extend the left skirt placket and align its edge to the fold edge of the left bodice facing foldline. Wrap the bodice facing around the skirt placket to the right side. On the right side of the back opening, fold the skirt placket to the inside and align the fold edge to the remaining back bodice facing foldline. Again, wrap the bodice facing around the skirt placket to the right side.

12 Stitch a $\frac{1}{2}$" (1.3 cm) seam. Trim and finish. When you flip the bodice up, the bodice facing will flip to the inside and align with the skirt placket.

13 Sew three buttonholes to the right back yoke edge and three buttons to left back yoke edge.

Little Boy Blue

A Christening Gown for Baby Boy

DESIGNED BY THE LATE ELIZABETH RHODES AND SUE STEWART

INSTRUCTIONS BY KATHY BARNARD

*T*HE TAILORED PRECISION OF SHARK'S TEETH, also called prairie points, lends elegance to a boy's gown without it looking overly frilly. And while tradition advocates white as the christening color of choice, pale blue is a charming option for a baby boy.

This picture of perfection was designed by the late Elizabeth Rhodes for her grandson, Hunter Michael. Elizabeth served as director of the Kent State School of Fashion Design and Merchandising for 15 years. She co-authored the book *Vintage Baby* with Martha Pullen and Sue Hausmann.

What You'll Need...

PATTERN
(available on the CD-rom)

"Little Boy Blue Christening Gown" (sizes NB to 18 mos.)

Gown

Center panel template

Shark's teeth template

Layout guides

Size chart

Armhole guide

FABRIC
(size chart, layout guide, and cutting dimensions provided on the CD-rom)

3¾ yd (3.4 m) of Nelona Swiss batiste

LACE AND TRIM

9½ yd (8.7 m) of single-loop tatted insertion (A)

3½ yd (3.2 m) of wide tatted insertion (B)

2½ yd (2.3 m) of triple-loop tatted edging (C)

9½ yd (8.7 m) of entredeux

SUPPLIES

60 or 80 wt fine cotton sewing thread (color to match batiste and white)

Size 60 machine needle

Size 70 machine needle

Wash-out basting glue (for shark's teeth)

Three ¼" (6 mm) mother-of-pearl buttons

Fine-tipped blue wash-away marking pen

Lace-shaping pinning board (optional)

FINISHED GARMENT

Gown finishes 48" (122 cm) from the top of the back neck to the end of the tatted edging hem. NOTE: *Soak all tatting and entredeux in water to preshrink. Hang to dry and press while slightly damp. Prewash fabric and dry in a dryer on low setting. Starch and press fabric well.*

How to Make It...

The basic construction for this gown is provided here. The specific technique instructions for creating shark's teeth (the pyramids of points along the center panel), and technique instructions for joining lace to lace, lace to entredeux, and entredeux to fabric, are in the Techniques section on page 124.

Follow the layout guide on the CD-rom to cut blocks and pattern pieces. The front yoke will be cut from a block of tucked fabric. Keep in mind that each ½" (1.3 cm) tuck requires 1" (2.5 cm) of fabric. The shark's teeth blocks for the center front skirt panel, the skirt hem, and the yoke are cut longer to accommodate the many rows of tucks required. Mark each shark's teeth block with its section number for easy reference later.

Prepare Lace

It is best to join the laces and entredeux first so that they are ready to insert when you need them. Set up machine with a size 70 needle and white 60 to 80 wt thread. Set machine for a narrow zigzag (L=1.0; W=2.5).

Narrow Insertion

Used on the sides of the skirt panel and the bottom of the yoke.

1 Cut one 91" (234 cm) strip of single-loop tatting (A) and two 91" (234 cm) strips of entredeux.

2 Trim the fabric seam tape along one side of each entredeux strip, leaving one side remaining.

3 Butt the header edge of the tatting to the trimmed edge of the entredeux and join with a zigzag. Repeat so that you have entredeux stitched to each side of the tatting (A) with seam tape remaining on both sides **(FIG. 1)**.

Wide Insertion

Used to join the shark's teeth blocks in the center panel.

1 Cut one 84" (213 cm) strip of single-oop tatting (A), one 84" (213 cm) strip of entredeux, and one 42" (106.5 cm) strip of wide tatted insertion (B).

2 Trim the fabric seam tape along one side of the entredeux strip, leaving one side remaining.

3 Butt the header edge of the tatting (A) to the trimmed edge of the entredeux and join with a zigzag.

Cut this 84" (213 cm) strip in half to make two 42" (106.5 cm) strips.

4 Butt the header edge of the tatting (A) to the header edge of wide tatted insertion (B). Repeat so that the wide tatted insertion (B) has a row of tatting (A) and entredeux on each side. The fabric seam tape should remain on both sides **(FIG. 2)**. This will be cut in shorter sections to join the center panel later.

Hem Edging

Used on the bottom of the gown skirt.

1 Cut one 76" (193 cm) strip of wide tatted insertion (B), one 76" (193 cm) strip of triple-loop tatted edging (C), one 76" (193 cm) strip of entredeux, and two 76" (193 cm) strips of single-loop tatting (A).

2 Join both strips of the tatting (A) to each side of the wide tatted insertion (B) using the same method as above.

3 Butt the header edge of the triple loop tatted edging (C) to one side of the joined strips from Step 2.

FIGURE 1

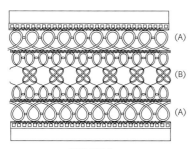

FIGURE 2

4 Trim the fabric seam tape along one side of the entredeux strip, leaving one side remaining.

5 Join the remaining header edge of the tatting (A) to the trimmed edge of the entredeux to complete the skirt edging strip. The fabric seam tape should remain on the other side of the entredeux **(FIG. 3)**.

Prepare Shark's Teeth Panels

A template for the largest shark's teeth pyramid is provided on CD-rom. Each consecutive smaller pyramid can be made from this template by counting the rows of tuck foldlines starting from the top and working down. Precision is key in creating neat rows of shark's teeth. Take extra time to measure and mark each tuck line accurately and neatly. When stitching tucks, set a guide on your machine to follow along the fold edge so that each tuck is the same width for the entire length of the tuck. Use the

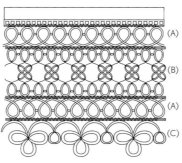

FIGURE 3

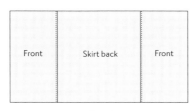

FIGURE 4

edge of a presser foot and move your needle if your machine allows, or place a piece of tape on the throat plate, or use your favorite method for setting stitch width guides to create an accurate ½" (1.3 cm) stitch width. If your tucks are greater than or less than ½" (1.3 cm), your points will not fold neatly into triangles.

Skirt Bottom

NOTE: *Please test your marking pen on a scrap of fabric. Starch the scrap first, mark, iron, then rinse. Iron the scrap dry. If the marks were easily removed, continue; if not, try changing markers and repeat the test.*

1 With a finished ¼" (6 mm) French seam (½" [1.3 cm] total seam), join the skirt front side panels to each side of the back skirt piece (back skirt must finish 35" [89 cm] from side seam to side seam). The center front will remain open **(FIG. 4)**. Starch and press the bottom of the skirt so that it is slightly stiff. (Starch helps protect the fabric from the marking pen and creates a crisp fold to follow.)

2 With the wash-out marking pen, mark the first tuck foldline 1⅝" (4 cm) from the bottom raw edge of the skirt. Mark all the way across the full length of the skirt front panels and back panel.

3 Trace the top portion of the shark's teeth template provided on the CD-rom to heavy paper or pattern stock. Stop at the sixth foldline.

4 Place the fabric on a pinning board. Slide the traced template under the fabric to the right side of the seam (on the skirt back). Begin marking from the side seam. Align the sixth horizontal foldline (bottom line of template) to the line drawn on the skirt. Align the first vertical clip on the bottom of the pyramid ½" (1.3 cm) from

the skirt seamline (**FIG. 5**). Smooth the fabric over the template (do not stretch taut) and pin to secure (keep bottom foldlines straight and aligned). Trace the foldlines and the clip lines onto the fabric. Shift the template to the left of the seam (on the front skirt panel) and realign the horizontal foldlines along the bottom. Align the last vertical clip on the bottom of the pyramid I" (2.5 cm) from the previously marked pyramid (**SEE FIG. 5**).

5 Continue shifting and connecting the pyramids keeping I" (2.5 cm) distance between the outermost clip lines on the bottom row of the pyramid. Mark from the side seam toward the center front on each side panel, and from the side seam to the side seam on the back. There should be six pyramids on the back skirt, and two pyramids on each side front skirt panel.

6 Refer to page I26 for detailed sharks teeth instructions. Fold and stitch each tuck on the foldline working from bottom up. Press all the tucks down. Working one row at a time, starting with the bottom row, accurately clip along the clip lines to the stitching, fold the points, glue-baste the points, and stitch the shark's teeth with a pin stitch. Complete an entire row before moving up to the next row. Repeat until all the rows of the shark's teeth are stitched. Use a narrow pin stitch with a size 60 machine needle and fine sewing thread (color to match fabric). Stitch on top of the tuck stitching line with the swing of the stitch biting toward the shark's teeth (pointing down). This stitch secures the points in place (**FIG. 6**).

7 When all the rows are complete, soak the skirt to remove the markings. Hang dry. Starch and press well. Set the skirt aside for later construction.

Center Front Panel

The center front skirt panel has four sections of shark's teeth, each section larger than the next. Each shark's teeth fabric block has been marked with a number, with #1 being the top, smallest section (see the Layout Guide). You will use the same shark's teeth template for each block by tracing only the number of tuck foldlines and clipping the lines specified for each block.

1 Starch and press each block until it is slightly stiff.

2 Tape the template to the pinning board.

3 Fold the fabric blocks in half lengthwise and crease to mark the center. With a marking pen, draw a line $1\frac{5}{8}$" (4 cm) from the bottom raw edge of each fabric block. Working with one block at a time, smooth the block over the template on the pinning board and align the centers and the bottom marked line of the fabric to the specified foldline on the template (**FIG. 7**).

Block #1 – 6 tucks (align to foldline 6)

Block #2 – 8 tucks (align to foldline 8)

Block #3 – 10 tucks (align to foldline 10)

Block #4 – 12 tucks (align to foldline 12)

4 Pin the fabric to the pinning board and carefully trace the foldlines and clip marks.

5 Fold and stitch each tuck on the foldline working from the bottom up. Press all the tucks down. Clip along the clip lines to the stitching, fold the points, glue-baste the points, and stitch the shark's teeth with a pin stitch one row at a time starting with the bottom row. Complete an entire row before moving up to the next row.

6 Complete all four blocks and soak to remove the pen marks. Lay flat to dry. Starch and press well. Set aside for later construction.

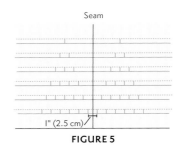

FIGURE 5

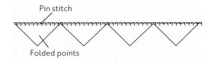

FIGURE 6

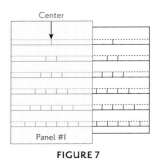

FIGURE 7

Gown Construction

All seams are noted on the pattern. Pay close attention, as the seams are different widths. A basic knowledge of garment construction is assumed.

At this point, you should have:

• A 42" (106.5 cm) strip of wide joined lace insertion for the center panel (entredeux on both sides).

• Four completed shark's teeth blocks.

• A 91" (231 cm) strip of narrow tatted insertion (entredeux on both sides).

• A skirt with shark's teeth stitched along the bottom.

• A 76" (193 cm) strip of joined lace for hem edging (entredeux on one side).

• A fabric block for front yoke.

• A fabric block for top of center panel.

- Two cut out sleeves.
- Two cut out back yokes.
- Four 17" (43 cm) bias strips (three 2" [5 cm] wide and one 1¼" [3.2 cm] wide).
- A 1" × 10" (2.5 × 25.5 cm) skirt placket strip.

Yoke

1 Starch and press the front yoke block. Mark a line across the block 1½" (3.8 cm) from the bottom edge. Mark three more lines above this line each 1¼" (3.2 cm) apart (**FIG. 8**).

2 Press along each foldline and stitch ½" (1.3 cm) from the fold edge to complete four ½" (1.3 cm) tucks across the front yoke block.

3 Place the yoke pattern on top of the tucked block. Align the top tuck stitching line at least 1" (2.5 cm) below the neck seamline. Trace the outline of the yoke. Cut out the sides, neck and shoulders only, leaving the bottom point design uncut (**FIG. 9**).

4 Join the back yokes to the front yoke along the shoulder seams with a ⅛" (3 mm) finished French seam. Refer to the Techniques section on page 124 if needed.

5 To make the Madeira border around the neck, press under ¼" (6 mm) along one long edge of the 1¼" (3.2 cm) wide bias strip (try not to stretch the bias as you press). Shape the bias strip into a circle with the fold edge to the outside; lightly starch and press. Lay the front and back yoke out flat on an ironing board and mark 1" (2.5 cm) from the cut edge of the neck using a marking pen. Place the bias to the neck edge and align the fold edge of the bias to the marked 1" (2.5 cm) line. Glue- or hand-baste along the fold edge to hold it in

place temporarily. Set the machine for a pin stitch using size 60 needle and colored fine thread. Stitch along the edge of the bias with the swing of the stitch biting into the bias (**FIG. 10**). NOTE: *The neck binding will be added at the end of the construction process.*

6 Cut a 12" (30.5 cm) strip from narrow entredeux and tatted insertion. Trim off the fabric seam tape from both sides. Pin the yoke to a lace-shaping board, right side facing up, and shape insertion along the bottom traced template line: Cut the insertion into four sections and place them along the bottom marked template line on the front yoke. Overlap the sections at the corners and center point (the top entredeux edge should overlap at the corners and the point by one entredeux hole). (These "miters" will be trimmed and whipped with a zigzag later to neaten them). Set the machine with a narrow zigzag (L=1.0; W=2.5) and fine white thread. With the right side facing up, zigzag over the edge of the entredeux so that the needle swings into the holes of the entredeux on one side and into the yoke fabric on the other side. You will be stitching on top of the tucks (**FIG. 11**).

7 Turn the yoke over, trim the excess fabric to ½" (1.3 cm) below the stitching line. Press the fabric up away from the lace and entredeux (clip the corners to the stitching to release). With the right side facing up, zigzag once more over the edge of the entredeux. Turn the yoke over and trim the excess fabric as close to the stitching as possible (**FIG. 12**).

8 Trim the angles at the points and corners carefully and whip by hand or by machine zigzag stitch (**FIG. 13**).

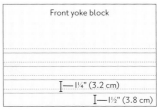

Front yoke block

1¼" (3.2 cm)

1½" (3.8 cm)

FIGURE 8

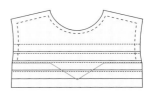

FIGURE 9

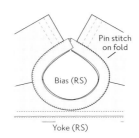

Pin stitch on fold

Bias (RS)

Yoke (RS)

FIGURE 10

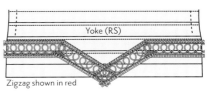

Yoke (RS)

Zigzag shown in red

FIGURE 11

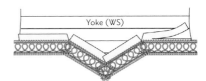

Yoke (WS)

FIGURE 12

FIGURE 13

Skirt

1 Set up the machine with a size 70 needle and fine white thread.

2 Assemble the center front panel: Trim the top of each shark's teeth block so that ¾" (2 cm) is left above the top line of stitching. Arrange the shark's teeth blocks from largest to smallest starting from the bottom. Using strips of wide, joined, tatted insertion, join the blocks together matching the centers and using the entredeux-to-fabric method. Roll and whip each seam. The section should finish with wide tatted insertion at the top (**FIG. 14**).

3 Join the remaining 7" × 13½" (18 × 34.5 cm) fabric block to the top edge of the entredeux.

4 Press the center panel block. Place the center panel pattern piece on top of the block, aligning the centers and bottom edge; cut out (**FIG. 15**).

5 Join a row of narrow tatting and entredeux insertion to each side of the center panel using the entredeux-to-fabric method. Trim the seam and roll and whip to finish.

6 Place the center panel pattern to the front cut edge of the skirt and cut the angle; be sure to leave a ½" (1.3 cm) seam allowance and align it so that the seamline falls on the edge of the shark's teeth pyramid (**FIG. 16**).

7 Join the center panel to the skirt front angled edges using the entredeux-to-fabric method. Trim the seams and roll and whip to finish.

8 Fold the skirt on the side seams and press flat. Place the armhole curve template to the top skirt corner; align the edge of the template to the seam fold and the top to the raw edges of the skirt (**FIG. 17**). Trace the curve and cut out (**FIG. 18**).

9 Fold the front skirt on the center with right sides together and stitch a tuck following the seamline at the entredeux edge (stitch in the ditch of the entredeux seam). Stop stitching and tie off 1¾" (4.5 cm) from the top (**FIG. 19**). Press the tuck open on the wrong side.

10 Using a long basting stitch, run five rows of gathering stitches across

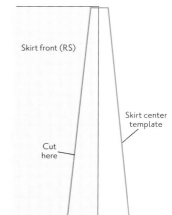

Skirt front (RS)

Skirt center template

Cut here

Leave ½" (1.3 cm) for seam

FIGURE 16

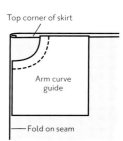

Top corner of skirt

Arm curve guide

Fold on seam

FIGURE 17

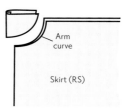

Arm curve

Skirt (RS)

FIGURE 18

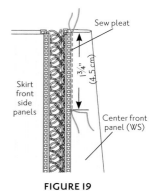

Sew pleat

Skirt front side panels

1¾" (4.5 cm)

Center front panel (WS)

FIGURE 19

#1

#2

#3

#4

FIGURE 14

FIGURE 15

the top of the front skirt. Start the first row ½" (1.3 cm) below the raw fabric edge. Stitch each consecutive row below the first, ⅜" (1 cm) apart running from the center insertion seam to the side seam.

11 Tie off the threads at the center and pull up the gathers to equal the width of the front yoke. Pin the skirt to the pinning board so that the top edge is perfectly straight **(FIG. 20)**. Place the yoke on top of the gathers aligning the edge of the entredeux to the top gathering row and point of the yoke to the center tuck seam. Glue-baste or pin and remove from the board. Zigzag along the entredeux edge through the gathers with the right side facing up **(FIG. 21)**.

12 Press the excess gathered skirt down away from the yoke. With the right side facing up, zigzag once more over the entredeux edge. Trim the excess gathered fabric from the wrong side close to the stitching. Remove the gathering threads and steam out the needle holes left behind. This completes the front.

13 Fold the back skirt panel in half to mark the center. Draw a 5" (12.5 cm)

line from the top raw edge along the center back for the placket (do not cut). With a 1.5 stitch length, stitch a V with the point of the V meeting the bottom of the line **(FIG. 22)**. Cut along the drawn line to open the V. Apply placket strip to slit (refer to Placket in the Techniques section on page 124 if needed).

14 Run two rows of gathering stitches ⅜" (1 cm) and ⅝" (1.5 cm) from the top edge of the back skirt. Stitch from the placket to the side seam on each side.

15 Press the back yoke facing to the inside ¾" (2 cm). Make a mark another ¾" (2 cm) from the fold (this is the second facing foldline). Pull the gathers in the back skirt to the equal width of the back yoke from the second facing foldline mark to the side edge. Wrap the facing around the skirt to the wrong side along the second foldline. With the right sides together, stitch a ½" (1.3 cm) seam. Stitch a second row of stitches ⅛" (3 mm) from the seam **(FIG. 23)**. Trim beside the second row of stitching and roll and whip ⅛" (3 mm) seam. Flip the yoke up and yoke facing to the inside. Press.

16 Apply the neck binding to finish the neck edge. Refer to Neck Binding in the Techniques section on page 124 if needed.

17 At the center of the sleeve, fold and baste a ¾" (2 cm) box tuck on the wrong side of the sleeve bottom edge, creating an A-line tuck on the right side **(FIG. 24)**.

18 Apply a bias binding in the same manner as the neck binding. Press a 1" (2.5 cm) bias strip in half. Place the bias to the sleeve bottom edge with the right sides together and raw edges even; stitch a precise ½" (1.3 cm) seam. (The sleeve allowance is ¼" [6 mm], however the binding will wrap over the seam, leaving ¼" [6 mm]). Trim the seam to a scant ¼" (6 mm). Press the binding down along the seam edge. With the binding extended, stitch the sleeve seam with a ⅛" (3 mm) finished French seam as on the shoulder seams (⅜" [1 cm] total seam). Wrap the binding over the bottom seam, matching the fold edge of the bias to the stitching line. Turn the sleeve wrong side out and hand-stitch the binding along the seamline **(FIG. 25)**.

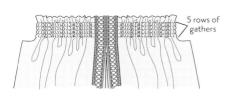

FIGURE 20

Yoke (RS)
Skirt (RS)
Zigzag shown in red

FIGURE 21

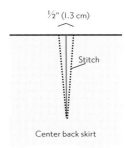

½" (1.3 cm)
Stitch
Center back skirt

FIGURE 22

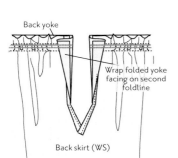

Back yoke
Wrap folded yoke facing on second foldline
Back skirt (WS)

FIGURE 23

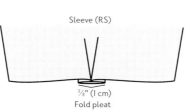

Sleeve (RS)
⅜" (1 cm)
Fold pleat

FIGURE 24

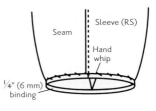

Sleeve (RS)
Seam
Hand whip
¼" (6 mm) binding

FIGURE 25

19 Run a row of ease stitches ⅜"
(1 cm) from the edge of the sleeve
cap. Gently pull the thread to
ease the sleeve cap (these are not
gathers). TIP: *If your sleeve will not
ease in neatly, fold a box tuck at the
center cap to take up the excess.* Set
the sleeve into the armholes with
right sides together. Hand-baste
in place matching the sleeve seam
to the skirt seam. Machine stitch
a ⅜" (1 cm) seam. Stitch again
⅛" (3 mm) from the seam into the
seam allowance. Trim the next to
the second row of stitching; roll
and whip the seam with a zigzag
to finish.

20 Mark and sew the three
buttonholes on the right side of
the back facing and three tiny ¼"
(6 mm) buttons on the left side.

21 Apply wide, joined, tatted edging
trim to the bottom raw edge of
the skirt: Pin the entredeux edge
to the fabric edge with right sides
together beginning at one side
seam. Leave ½" (1.3 cm) excess
at the side seam for seaming the
lace ends together later. Using the
entredeux-to-fabric method, join
the edging to the hem. When you
reach the open side seam, place
the lace ends right sides together,
and stitch a ½" (1.3 cm) seam.
Zigzag and trim the lace seam.
Finish the entredeux to the skirt
join. Press the edging down.

22 Soak the top of the dress in water
to remove the marks on the yoke.
Hang to dry. Starch and press the
entire dress.

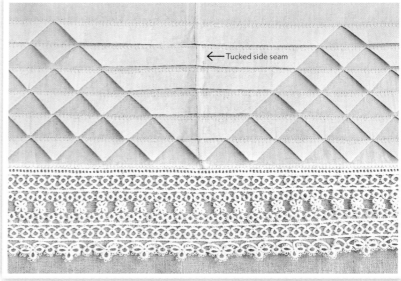

←Tucked side seam

SEWING FOR A
Little Princess

THE FIRST REQUIREMENT FOR A PRINCESS, of course, is a lovely dress. We selected four different designs each unique in fabrication, embellishment and style, and each inspired by vintage finery. The first is our take on a portrait dress worn by a 2-year-old Princess Margaret in 1934. Designer Janet Gilbert figured out how to make the pretty double-scalloped hemline to turn the *Sew Beautiful* "Pascale" pattern into a nearly identical version of the royal original. Our Elizabeth Red Dress was inspired by a vintage silk dress we found for $10 at an antiques store. With a V-shaped yoke and box-pleated front and back skirts, it's a little tailored treasure to suit any occasion. For the more advanced sewist, Lady Anna's cutwork dress will take your machine embroidery skills to a new level. The two-piece design, circa 1900, was purchased along London's Portobello Road, and the underdress is just as pretty made without the cutwork overlay. Princess Charlotte's Baby Dress and Bonnet ensemble was designed by Wendy Schoen. The exquisite handwork, including a detached appliqué dogwood flower, will have you stealing every moment you can to sit and stitch.

Princess Margaret Rose

BY JANET GILBERT

Princess Margaret Rose, 2, left, and Princess Elizabeth, 6, daughters of the Duke and Duchess of York, pose, August 20, 1934, London, England. Marcus Adams/Camera Press/Redux

*I*N 1934, WHEN 2-YEAR-OLD PRINCESS MARGARET ROSE posed for a portrait with her 6-year-old sister princess Elizabeth, the younger royal wore a dear little smocked dress that was finished at the bottom with what we are calling a double-scalloped hem. Leave it to Janet Gilbert to figure out the hem technique and reproduce the dress design for today's little princess. She also added an original smocking plate that opens up possibilities for adding more color; smock in a soft hue and make your slip from the same color batiste to shadow through the sheer organdy dress.

What You'll Need...

PATTERN
(available on the CD-rom)

"Margaret Rose Dress" (sizes 18 mos. to 4)

Smocking graph (on page 29)

Double-scallop hem template

FABRIC
(layout guides and yardage requirements provided on the CD-rom)

Italian organdy for dress

Satin batiste for slip

TRIM
Three ⅜" (1 cm) mother-of-pearl buttons

¾ yd (68.5 cm) piping cord for self-made piping

FLOSS
DMC Six-strand embroidery
  #3743 lt antique violet
  #3042 md antique violet
  #B5200 snow white

SUPPLIES
Small appliqué or duck-billed scissors (highly recommended)

Pattern tracing paper

Wash-away marking pen

Wash-away basting tape

Short ruler or seam gauge

Serrated blade scissors are best for cutting organdy

Bone folder (or similar tool)

Pinning board

FINISHED GARMENT

Size 18 mos.
20" (51 cm) around the chest
19"–20" (48.5–51 cm) around the waist
8" (20.5 cm) center back to waist

Size 2
21" (53.3 cm) around the chest
20" (51 cm) around the waist
8.5" (21.5 cm) center back to waist

Size 3
22" (56 cm) around the chest
20½" (52 cm) around the waist
9" (23 cm) center back to waist

Size 4
23" (58.4 cm) around the chest
21 (53.5 cm) around the waist
9.5" (24 cm) center back to waist

What to Cut...

(cutting charts provided on the CD-rom)

FROM ITALIAN ORGANDY

Two front yokes

Two full back bodices on fold

Two front tulip sleeves on fold

Two back tulip sleeves on fold

Skirt front

Skirt back

Two strips 7" (18 cm) × the width of skirt for scalloped hem band

Two strips 3½" (9 cm) × width of skirt for hem facing

Bias strips 1½" (3.8 cm) wide × 1" (2.5 cm) longer than neck measurement for binding

Bias strips cut 1½" (3.8 cm) wide for yoke seam and back bodice seam piping

CONSTRUCTION TIP: *When using sheer fabrics, use two layers of the fabric for self-fabric piping. This will prevent the piping cord from peeking through.*

FROM SATIN BATISTE

One full slip bodice front

Two slip bodice backs

Skirt front

Skirt back

How to Smock It...

Smocking Preparation
- Pleat nine full-space rows. Rows 1–9 are holding rows.
- Unpick a ½" (1.3 cm) seam allowance on each side. Tie off the skirt to the width of the front bodice minus 1" (2.5 cm; use the bodice pattern as a template).

- Optional—Backsmock top holding row with two strands of floss for ease in construction.

Smocking Notes
- Stitch all smocking with three strands of floss.
- Work hand embroidery after the smocking is complete.

- Count pleats and mark the center valley with a small safety pin or contrasting thread.

Smocking
Detailed instructions for basic smocking stitches are provided on page 138.

1 Starting on Row 1, one pleat to the left of center, stitch a cable

row starting with an up cable and #3743 (lt antique violet). Continue smocking to the end of the pleats. Invert your work and starting at the center, continue working the cable row to the other end.

2 Work an identical image cable row across Row 2.

3 Connect the two cable rows, with a two-step trellis with #3042 (md antique violet). Starting one pleat to the left of center on Row 2, stitch a down cable, two-step trellis up to Row 1. Continue the two-step trellis to the end of the pleats. Invert your work and starting at the center, continue stitching the two-step trellis to the other side.

4 Rows 6–7 are identical to Rows 1–2 (two cable rows connected with a two-step trellis).

5 Smocking on Rows 2½–3 is a thirteen cable stitch, two-step baby wave combination stitched with #3042 (md antique violet). On Row 2, starting seven pleats to the left of center, stitch thirteen cable stitches starting with a down cable. Next, stitch a two-step baby wave up to Row 2½. Continue the stitch combination to the end of

How to Embroider...

Embroidery

Stitch diagrams can be found in the Techniques section on page 124.

1 Work a single bullion rose in the center of alternating smocked hexagons. See graph for placement.

2 With a #9 sharp needle, work two parallel bullions with one strand of #3747 (lt antique violet). Each bullion is nine wraps and covers two pleats.

3 Work six bullions around the center bullions to form the petals. The outer bullions are stitched with one strand of #B520 (snow white) and are twelve wraps each.

4 Work four lazy daises with #3747 (lt antique violet) to create leaves. See graph for placement.

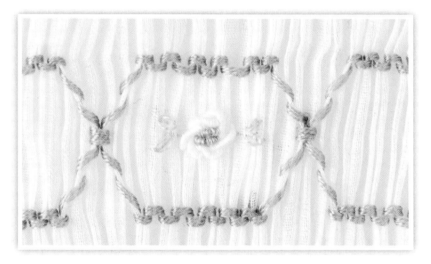

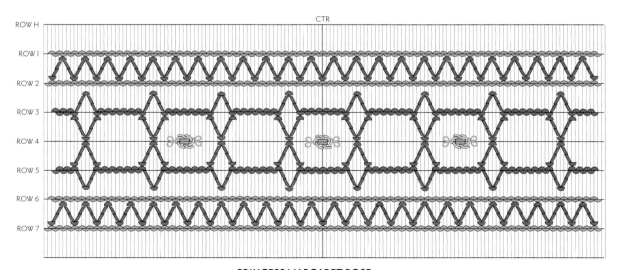

**PRINCESS MARGARET ROSE
SMOCKING GRAPH**

the pleats. Invert your work and continue stitching the combination to the other side.

6 Row 5–5½ is a mirror-image thirteen-cable stitch, two-step baby wave stitch combination.

7 Single two-step trellis chevrons are stitched toward Row 4 to create hexagons. See graph for placement.

8 Remove all pleating threads except the holding row. Block the smocking to the width of the bodice.

How to Make It...

Seam allowances are ½" (1.3 cm).

Dress Front

1 Cut the armhole curves in the smocked front. Place the lower bodice template to the top edge of the smocking and trace the curves with a fabric-marking pen. Zigzag stitch just inside the marked line and cut out the curves next to the stitching (**FIG. 1**).

2 Prepare piping by wrapping and stitching cord with a double layer of bias organdy.

3 Stitch piping to the bottom edge of one yoke layer. Press the seam back to the wrong side of the yoke and the piping down. Using wash-away basting tape, remove the paper from one side of the tape and fuse it to the piping seam on the wrong side of the yoke, positioning it close to the piping.

4 Pin the smocked skirt to a pinning board to block and straighten the top edge. Remove the paper from the basting tape on the back side of the yoke and fuse the top of the smocking, aligning the piped edge to the top cable row (**FIG. 2**). Finger press to fuse it in place.

5 Fold the yoke down to expose the seam. Pin the remaining organdy yoke lining to the wrong side of the smocked skirt and stitch the seam right next to the piped edge, catching all three layers in the seam (**FIG. 3**). Trim the seam to ¼" (6 mm) and zigzag.

6 Flip both yokes up and press the seam. Set the front aside.

Dress Back

1 Stitch the piping to half of the back bodice. Bend a corner in the end of the piping up toward the seam allowance at the center foldline (**FIG. 4**). Repeat for both bodices and set aside.

2 Stitch a placket in the center back skirt; refer to Placket in the Techniques section on page 124.

3 Run gathering stitches in the top edge of the back skirt and gather the skirt on each side of the placket to fit the piped half of the back bodice from the side seam to the foldline. NOTE: *The left side of the skirt placket will remain extended and aligned with the center foldline of the back bodice. The right side of the skirt placket will fold under, and the fold edge will align to the foldline of the opposite back bodice.*

4 With right sides together, pin the skirt to the back bodice. Wrap the back bodice lining layer around through the placket and pin to the wrong side of the skirt so that the skirt is sandwiched between the bodice layers and the placket edge meets the foldline of the bodice

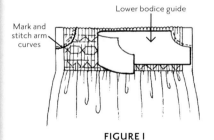

FIGURE 1

Mark and stitch arm curves
Lower bodice guide

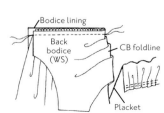

FIGURE 2

Tape
Yoke (RS)
Piping

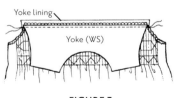

FIGURE 3

Yoke lining
Yoke (WS)

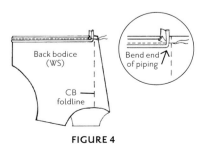

FIGURE 4

Back bodice (WS)
Bend end of piping
CB foldline

FIGURE 5

Bodice lining
Back bodice (WS)
CB foldline
Placket

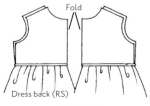

FIGURE 6

Fold
Dress back (RS)

(FIG. 5). Stitch the seam. Trim the seam to ¼" (6 mm) and zigzag.

5 Flip the back bodices up and press the seam **(FIG. 6)**. Set the back aside.

Sleeves

1 The sleeve sections were cut on the fold and will remain folded (treat as one layer). Place one front and one back together, back section overlapping front section. Align the center mark and stay-stitch through all layers within the seam allowance. Repeat in mirror image to create the opposite

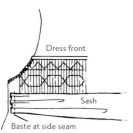

FIGURE 7

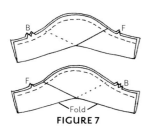

FIGURE 8

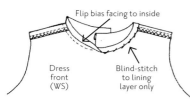

FIGURE 9

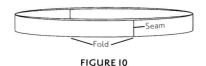

FIGURE 10

sleeve so that you have a right and left sleeve **(FIG. 7)**.

2 Run an ease stitch in the sleeve cap on the seamline. Pull to ease the sleeve and cup it slightly. Set the sleeves aside.

Sash

1 Fold the sash in half lengthwise and stitch one long edge and one end.

2 Turn the sash through the open end and press. Set aside.

Assembly

1 Separate the yokes and bodices at the shoulders and stitch the front bodice layer to the back bodice layer and lining to lining at the shoulder seams. NOTE: *This might take a little twisting, but it is not hard to do.* To finish the seams, stitch again ⅛" (3 mm) from the seam stitching. Trim the seam next to the second row of stitching.

2 Gather the raw ends of the sashes and baste them to the front smocked dress along the sides seams with the bottom edge of the sash aligned to the last row of smocking **(FIG. 8)**.

3 Stitch the front to the back at the side seams using a French seam. Or, stitch a regular seam, trim, and then roll and whip to finish.

4 Finish the neckline with a bias binding, stitching a precise ½" (6 mm) to apply **(FIG. 9)**. Refer to Bias Binding in the Techniques section on page 124.

5 Pin the sleeves to the armholes with the right sides together; stitch a ½" (2.5 cm) seam. Stitch ⅛" (3 mm) from the seam and trim the seam allowance along the second row of stitching. Overcast the edge with a narrow zigzag to finish. Press the seam.

6 Sew three buttonholes in the right side of the bodice ½" (2.5 cm) from the fold edge.

7 Mark and stitch the buttonholes as indicated on the pattern on the left back bodice edge.

8 Sew on the buttons corresponding to the buttonholes.

Double-Scalloped Hem

There are three pieces involved when creating a double-scalloped hem. For illustration purposes each piece is shown in a different color.

- The dress skirt
- The facing
- The bottom scallop band

Prepare Bottom Scallop Band

1 Seam the skirt hem band strips together end-to-end to form a ring.

2 Double check that the seamed circle matches the exact circumference of the dress skirt. Adjust the seam allowance if needed.

3 Trim the seam allowances to ¼" (6 mm) and press open.

4 Fold the fabric strip ring in half (right sides together) to create a 3½" (9 cm) wide double-layer ring **(FIG. 10)**.

5 Match up the seam allowances and finger press to mark the center front and center back of the ring.

6 Since each skirt may be slightly different, you will need to adjust the scallops to fit. If the adjustment is slight, you can make the scallops at the side seams slightly larger or smaller and it will not be noticeable. Or, you may want to adjust the width of your scallop template so that all of your scallops are precisely the same size and fit evenly within your circumference. Trace the scallop template onto the

pattern-making material of your choice. We suggest using one long strip and repeat the template for the entire front/back of the skirt.

7 Pin the template to the organdy strip. Center the scallop template on the finger-pressed center. The bottom edge of the template needs to be at least ¼" (6 mm) away from the bottom foldline (**FIG. 11**). Trace the scallops with a wash-away marking pen.

8 With a short stitch length, stitch on your marked lines. Pivot at the point of each scallop.

9 Remove all the marked lines with cool, clear water. Press.

10 Trim the seam allowance to ⅛" (3 mm) (**FIG. 12**). Clip and notch the points (**FIG. 13**). Turn the hem band right side out and push the scallops out with the edge of a bone folder tool or a spoon. Press the scallops. Set the scalloped band aside.

Prepare Hem Facing

1 Seam 3½" (9 cm) facing strips end-to-end to form a ring.

2 Double check that the facing is the same circumference as the bottom hem band. Make adjustments to the seam allowance if needed.

3 Trim the seams to ¼" (6 mm) and press open.

Join Band and Facing

1 Pin the prepared scallop band to the wrong side of the facing. Match up the top edges and the seamlines (**FIG. 14**).

2 With the scallop band facing up (**SEE FIG. 14**), trace a scallop that is ¾" (2 cm) above the bottom edge of the scalloped band seam with a wash-away marking pen and a

short ruler or hem gauge. Double-check that the points match up and the width is correct and make adjustments if needed.

3 With a short stitch length, stitch on your marked line.

4 Remove all the marked lines with cool, clear water. Press out the water in a towel and then iron dry.

5 Trim the top seam allowance down to ⅛" (3 mm) (**FIG. 15**).

6 Flip the strip so that the facing side is face up. Trace a scallop that is ⅜" (1 cm) below the topstitching line with a wash-away marking pen and a short ruler or seam gauge (**FIG. 16**). This line indicates how much the two scallops will overlap.

7 Double-check that the points match up and the width is correct. Make adjustments if needed.

Join Band/Facing to Dress

1 Pin the bottom scallop/facing to the right side of the dress skirt (**FIG. 17**). Match up the bottom edges and side seams.

2 Carefully shifting top scallop out of the way, stitch just the facing to the dress skirt along the marked lines with a short stitch length (**FIG. 18**). This stitching line is the bottom edge of the top scallop.

3 Double-check your stitching lines to ensure the points are sharp and they line up. Make correction if needed.

4 Remove all the marked lines with cool, clear water.

5 Press the stitching line.

6 Trim the seam allowance down to ⅛" (3 mm) (**FIG. 19**).

7 Flip the seam out and push out the scallops so that they lay on the

right sides over the bottom scallop band and the seam is enclosed between the facing and the skirt layers. NOTE: *At this point it's going to look a little confusing until all the pieces are going in the correct direction* (**FIG. 20**). Finger press the bottom seamline of the top scallop. Tuck the points of the bottom scallop band under the top scallop.

8 Once finger pressed and neatened, press with steam iron.

9 From the back, hand pick stitch the bottom scallop band to the dress enclosing the raw edges (**FIG. 21**).

Slip Instructions

1 Sew the front bodice to the back bodice along the shoulder seams. Repeat for the lining.

2 Place the lining to the bodice with right sides together; stitch the back seams, neck and arm curves (**FIG. 22**). Trim the seams and clip the curves. Turn by pulling the backs through the front. Press the seams flat. Set the bodice aside.

3 Sew a placket in the center back of the slip skirt. Refer to Placket in the Techniques section on page 124.

4 Run two rows of gathering stitches in the top edge of the front skirt and back skirt.

5 Gather the front skirt to fit the front bodice and back skirt to fit the back bodices. Sew the waist seam, treating both layers of the bodice as one. Trim the seam and finish. Press the waist seam up.

6 Sew the side seams of the front and back skirt and bodice with right sides together. Trim the seams and finish the edges.

7 Hem the slip so that it does not fall below the scallop peaks.

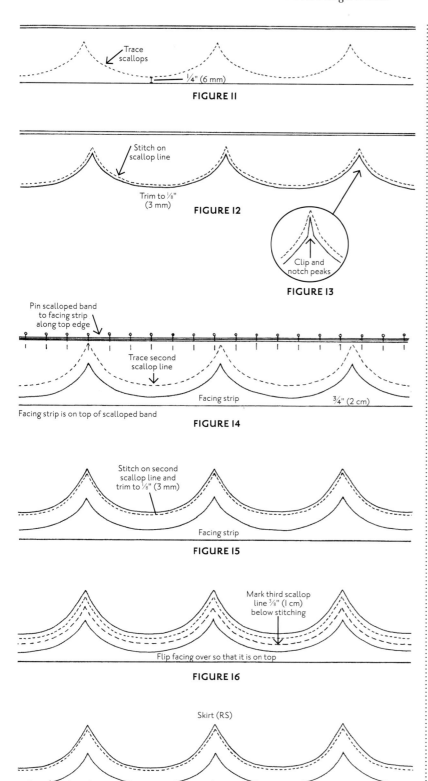

Trace scallops

¼" (6 mm)

FIGURE 11

Stitch on scallop line

Trim to ⅛" (3 mm)

FIGURE 12

Clip and notch peaks

FIGURE 13

Pin scalloped band to facing strip along top edge

Trace second scallop line

Facing strip

¾" (2 cm)

Facing strip is on top of scalloped band

FIGURE 14

Stitch on second scallop line and trim to ⅛" (3 mm)

Facing strip

FIGURE 15

Mark third scallop line ⅜" (1 cm) below stitching

Flip facing over so that it is on top

FIGURE 16

Skirt (RS)

Pin facing edge to bottom of skirt

FIGURE 17

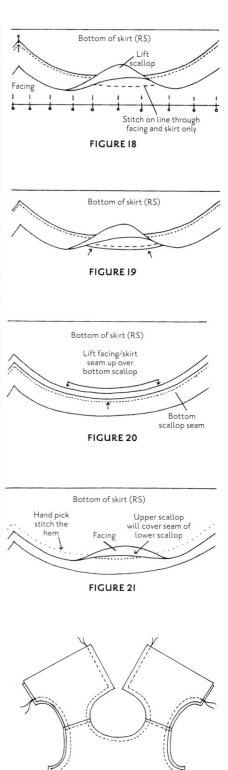

Bottom of skirt (RS)

Lift scallop

Facing

Stitch on line through facing and skirt only

FIGURE 18

Bottom of skirt (RS)

FIGURE 19

Bottom of skirt (RS)

Lift facing/skirt seam up over bottom scallop

Bottom scallop seam

FIGURE 20

Bottom of skirt (RS)

Hand pick stitch the hem

Upper scallop will cover seam of lower scallop

Facing

FIGURE 21

FIGURE 22

Lady Anna

*L*ONG BEFORE MARTHA PULLEN had grandchildren of her own, she spotted this antique dress, circa 1900, along Portobello Road in London. Her own children were long out of heirloom clothing, so she tucked the lovely garment among her collection. Only after she developed her antique cutwork machine embroidery CDs did she remember the little dress.

Using designs available on the CD-rom included in this book, Sue Stewart reproduced an heirloom dress that very closely resembles the original. The reproduction, as pictured is made of cotton lawn. Although the fabric was selected in keeping with the delicate nature of the antique, Sue noted difficulty in machine embroidering on it. She suggests using Nelona Swiss batiste for a machine-embroidered reproduction and cotton lawn for hand embroidery.

What You'll Need...

PATTERN
(available on the CD-rom)

"Lady Anna's Antique Reproduction Dress" (sizes 2 to 4)

FABRIC
(size and cutting charts, layout guides, and yardage requirements provided on the CD-rom)

Nelona Swiss batiste or cotton lawn

TRIMS (ALL SIZES)

2½ yd (2.3 m) entredeux (with ½" [1.3 cm] wide seam tape)

3¾ yd (3.4 m) of ⅝" (1.5 cm) wide French lace edging

THREAD

White Madeira Tanne 80 wt fine thread for heirloom sewing

Mettler 60 wt cotton for a delicate matte finish embroidery thread, or 40 wt rayon for a slight sheen

Pearl cotton size 12 for corded pintucks and scalloped edges

EMBROIDERY
(available on the CD-rom)

Cutwork Design

SUPPLIES

Size 1.6/80 twin needle for pintucks

Size 60 to 70 universal needle for construction

Sulky Solvy water-soluble stabilizer medium weight

Six ½" (1.3 cm) mother-of-pearl buttons

Blue wash-away marking pen

7-groove pintuck foot

Cording foot

NOTE: *Slightly more yardage is required for making this dress with machine embroidery due to the excess needed for hooping. The CD-rom provides layout and yardage guides for both options, with or without machine embroidery; be sure to select the correct guide for the type of dress you are making.*

FINISHED GARMENT

Size 2
21" (53.5 cm) across chest
20½" (52 cm) around waist
8½" (21.5 cm) center back to waist

Size 3
22" (56 cm) across chest
21" (53.5 cm) around waist
9" (23 cm) center back to waist

Size 4
23" (58.5 cm) across chest
21½" (54.5 cm) around waist
9½" (24 cm) center back to waist

How to Make It...

Preparation

Seam allowances are ½" (1.3 cm) unless otherwise noted.

Trace pieces 1, 2, 3, 4, 5, 6, 7, and the arm curve template for the skirt from the CD-rom to pattern paper.

Prewash the fabric laces and entredeux before cutting out. Press the fabric with a steam iron, but do not starch unless instructed.

To leave adequate space for hooping machine embroidery designs, the Sleeve (5) and Overlay (3 and 4) pieces are traced onto blocks of fabric and cut out after the embroidery is complete. For this application, follow the "With Machine Embroidery" layout guide. In the same manner, a rectangle of fabric is pintucked for the front and back yokes before the pieces are cut out. This will be the method used for both options. If not using machine embroidery, follow the "Without Machine Embroidery" layout guide.

FOR PINTUCKED YOKE AND CUFFS

Cut blocks of fabric for the front (1) and back (2) yokes according to the cutting chart given on the CD-rom. The rectangles are shown as 1a and 2b on the layout.

The cuff piece (6) is drafted with allowance for five tucks to be stitched horizontally, so the pintucks will be added to the cuffs after they are cut out.

Seam allowances are ½" (1.3 cm).

Yoke

Press the fabric rectangle with a steam iron. <u>Do not starch the fabric</u> until instructed to do so.

1 Set up your machine with a 1.6/80 twin needle, Madeira 80 wt thread and 7-groove pintuck foot. Set a 1.5 stitch length. Set the tension slightly higher than normal. Place size 12 pearl cotton in the center groove of the foot and pull out a 2" (5 cm) tail. The cord will ride between the needles and under the fabric as you stitch. Test on a scrap of fabric before pintucking the yoke rectangle.

2 For the front yoke rectangle, pull a thread about ½" (1.3 cm) from the edge of the rectangle to find straight grain. Stitch the first twin needle pintuck along this pulled line.

3 Stitch the next pintuck ¼" (6 mm) away from the first. Set your needle position so that the pintucks can be guided easily inside the foot grooves. Stitch slowly and carefully to ensure evenly spaced, straight, vertical tucks (precision is important). Continue stitching ¼" (6 mm) spaced tucks until you reach the end of the rectangle.

4 While the machine is set for pintucks, stitch five corded pintucks in each sleeve cuff. Mark the lengthwise center with a crease and stitch the first tuck on the center. Stitch two more evenly spaced tucks on each side of the center placing them ¼" (6 mm) apart.

5 Block the tucked fabric so that the pintucks are straight. Use a pinning board and steam to help you achieve straight, vertical pintucks. Now you may starch and press your pintucked fabric. Set the cuffs aside.

6 Place the front yoke pattern (1) on top of the pintucked fabric and cut out **(FIG. 1)**.

7 For the back yoke rectangles, pull a thread 2" (5 cm) from the selvage or straight raw edge. Stitch the first pintuck along this line. Continue stitching vertical pintucks ¼" (6 mm) apart until you reach the end of the rectangle.

8 To the edge of fabric, align the straight edge of the back yoke pattern (2) with the center back line (indicated on the pattern) ⅝" (1.5 cm) from the first tuck. Cut out **(FIG. 2)**. Repeat for the other side in mirror image.

9 Change the machine to a single size 60 or 70 sewing needle. Join the yoke along the shoulder seams with a ¼" (6 mm) French seam (total ½" [1.3 cm] seam allowance).

10 Cut a strip of entredeux 1" (2.5 cm) longer than the neckline circumference. Trim the seam tape from one side of the entredeux (this will be for the lace edging).

11 Pin the entredeux to the right side of the yoke neck with the edge of the seam tape to the edge of the neck and stitch right along entredeux edge (stitch in the ditch) using a ½" (1.3 cm) seam **(FIG. 3)**.

12 Trim the seam to ⅛" (3 mm) and set the machine for a narrow zigzag (L=1.0; W=4.5). Set the tension slightly higher than normal. Stitch along the seam to roll and whip. This requires the swing of the needle to enter next to the entredeux on the straight stitch line and swing off past the seam edge. Setting the tension slightly higher helps to draw up the fabric to "roll" the seam **(FIG. 4)**. Trim the entredeux ends even with the edge of the back yoke (the facing is not folded at this time). Press the seam down away from

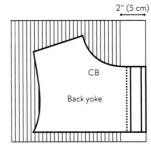

FIGURE 1

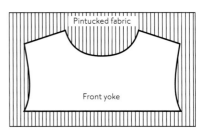

FIGURE 2

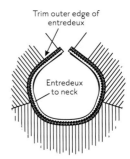

FIGURE 3

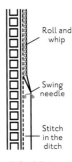

FIGURE 4

the entredeux. To secure, straight stitch or zigzag over the seam (**FIG. 5**).

13 Cut a piece of lace edging twice the length of the neck circumference. Pull a header thread to gather the lace to the neck edge along the trimmed entredeux edge.

14 Butt the lace to the entredeux edge under the presser foot; zigzag together (**FIG. 6**).

15 Cut three strips of entredeux, one the width of the front yoke lower edge and two for the lower edges of the back yokes. Place the entredeux to the bottom edge of the yokes with the right sides together; stitch in the ditch. Trim the seam and roll and whip with a narrow zigzag (**FIG. 7**). Press the seam down away from the entredeux and straight-stitch or zigzag over the seam to secure (**SEE FIG. 5**).

16 Fold and press the back yoke facing under ¼" (6 mm), then again ¾" (2 cm). Straight-stitch along the fold edge to secure the facing. Zigzag across the entredeux at the neck edge and bottom edge to secure (**FIG. 8**). Set the pintucked yokes aside.

Skirt

1 Starch and press the skirt front. Mark the center of the front skirt with a wash-away marking pen. Using the machine embroidery download, select design mp2009 to create a linear pattern of cutwork for center front skirt. The pattern will be stitched twice— once as a mirror image to create a single motif (**FIG. 9**). The motif "set" will be stitched over and over down the skirt center front to form a long, vertical, cutwork design.

2 Set up the machine with an embroidery needle and Mettler 60 wt cotton or 40 wt rayon thread. Stitch out design mp2009 on a scrap of fabric to use as a template for placement. Hoop the skirt fabric with two layers of Solvy. Stitch out the first repeat and shift the fabric in the hoop to stitch out the second repeat. It is essential to use the template and note the positioning of the embroidery each time the fabric is shifted in the hoop. Continue until the entire center front skirt is embroidered. TIP: *Cut away, do not tear away the excess stabilizer before soaking, as tearing can pull the stitches on the cutwork.* Soak the embroidered skirt in water to remove all the stabilizer. Once dry, starch and press.

3 Set up your machine with Madeira 80 wt thread and size 60 or 70 needle. Mark the top of the skirt fabric for the center pleat 1¼" (3.2 cm) on each side of the center front line to equal a total width of 2½" (6.5 cm). Mark 1½" (3.8 cm) from each mark and bring marks together to form a ¾" (2 cm) pleat on each side of center (**FIG. 10**).

4 Make a mark ¾" (2 cm) from the fold edge of the first pleat and another 1½" (3.8 cm) away. Bring the marks together to make another ¾" (2 cm) pleat. Pleats will measure ¾" (2 cm) from fold to fold (**FIG. 11**).

5 Repeat this across each side of the skirt until you have five pleats on each side for all sizes, marking each pleat ¾" (2 cm) from the fold of the previous pleat and folding a ¾" (2 cm) pleat each time. Baste across pleats (**FIG. 12**).

6 Align the center of the yoke to the center of the pleated skirt top and mark each end of the yoke on the skirt (**FIG. 13**).

7 Using the template for the skirt armhole curves provided with pattern, align the curve with the

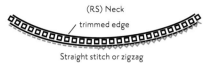

(RS) Neck
trimmed edge

Straight stitch or zigzag

Seam is pressed down away from
entredeux on wrong side

FIGURE 5

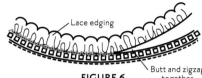

Lace edging

Butt and zigzag
together

FIGURE 6

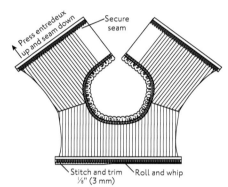

Press entredeux
up and seam down

Secure
seam

Stitch and trim
⅛" (3 mm)

Roll and whip

FIGURE 7

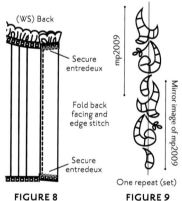

(WS) Back

Secure
entredeux

Fold back
facing and
edge stitch

Secure
entredeux

mp2009

Mirror image of mp2009

One repeat (set)

FIGURE 8   **FIGURE 9**

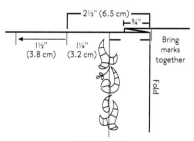

2½" (6.5 cm)

¾"

Bring
marks
together

1½"
(3.8 cm)

1¼"
(3.2 cm)

Fold

FIGURE 10

mark. Trace the armhole curve and side seam. Pull a thread along the side seam cutting line, from the top to the bottom of the skirt to create a straight line for cutting (**FIG. 14**). If the last tuck is caught in the armhole curve, straight-stitch along the curve first to secure the tuck, then cut out along the pulled line and the armhole curve (**FIG. 15**). *You may be removing a little fabric from each side of the skirt, but this is required for a custom fit to the yoke and will not affect the fit.*

8 Apply the placket to the back skirt; refer to Placket instructions in the Techniques section on page 124.

9 Fold the right side of the placket to the inside of the skirt; leave the left side extended.

10 On the right side, make a mark at the top of the skirt 1½" (3.8 cm) from the placket fold edge (**FIG. 16**). Bring this mark to the edge of the placket to create a ¾" (2 cm) pleat (**FIG. 17**).

11 From the fold of this pleat, make a mark 1⅛" (3 cm), then another mark 1½" (3.8 cm) from that mark. Bring the marks together to create a second ¾" (2 cm) pleat with the pleat folds spaced 1⅛" (3 cm) apart (**FIG. 18**). Continue to measure from each pleat fold 1⅛" (3 cm) and then 1½" (3.8 cm) from that mark to create four pleats on each side for sizes 2 and 3, and fold five pleats on each side for size 4.

12 For the left side, make a mark (a) ½" (1.3 cm) from the edge of the extended placket. Make another mark (b) 1½" (3.8 cm) from that mark (a) (**FIG. 19**). Bring these marks together to create a ¾" (2 cm) pleat. Repeat marking and pleating in the same manner as the right side.

17 Baste the pleats in place.

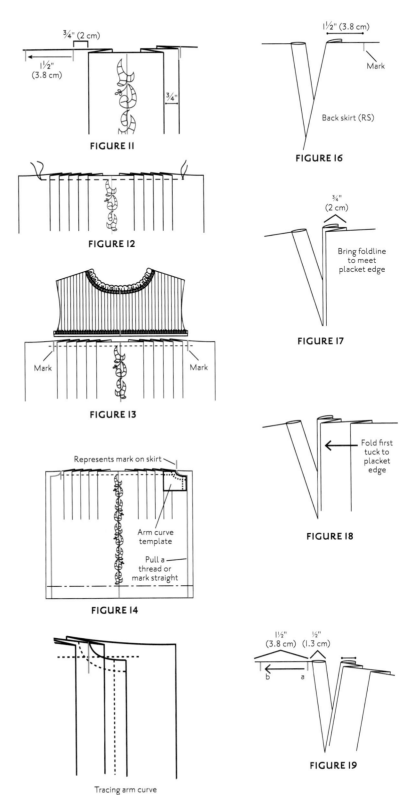

FIGURE 11

FIGURE 12

FIGURE 13

Represents mark on skirt

Arm curve template

Pull a thread or mark straight

FIGURE 14

Tracing arm curve
FIGURE 15

Mark

Back skirt (RS)

FIGURE 16

¾" (2 cm)

Bring foldline to meet placket edge

FIGURE 17

Fold first tuck to placket edge

FIGURE 18

FIGURE 19

18 Align the edge of the back yoke pattern to the placket edge of the pleated skirt top and mark each end of the yoke on the skirt (**FIG. 20**).

19 Using the template for the skirt armhole curves provided with the pattern, align the curve with the mark and trace the armhole curve and side seam. Pull a thread along the side seam cutting line from the top to the bottom of the skirt to create a straight line for cutting. If the last tuck is caught in the armhole curve, straight-stitch along the curve first to secure the tuck, then cut out along the pulled line and armhole curve (**SEE FIG. 15**).

20 Stitch the front skirt to the back skirt with a rolled and whipped seam or a French seam (both taking a total of ½" (1.3 cm) seam allowance. Refer to French Seam in the Techniques section on page 124. For the rolled and whipped seam, begin with a straight stitch along the ½" (1.3 cm) seamline. Trim the seam to ⅛" (3 mm) and set the machine for a narrow zigzag (L=1.0; W=4.5). Zigzag along the edge to roll and whip the seam close to the straight stitching. Set the skirt aside.

Overlay

1 Overlay pieces (3 and 4) should be traced on blocks of fabric large enough to hoop and embroider.

2 Set up your machine with an embroidery needle and Mettler 60 wt cotton or 40 wt rayon thread. Stitch out designs mp2007, mp2008, and mp2009 to use as a template for aligning embroidery to the overlays. Mark the back overlay pieces with mp2008 and mp2009. Reduce the size of the motif for smaller sized patterns if needed. Mark the motif centers on the overlays and hoop with two layers of stabilizer.

3 Stitch out the center front motif mp2007 first. Rehoop and align mp2008 and mp2009 to complete one side of the front. Repeat mp2008 and mp2009 on the other side in a mirror image. Cut away the excess stabilizer and set aside the front overlay.

4 Hoop the back overlay pieces (4) with two layers of stabilizer and stitch out mp2008 and mp2009. Mirror image and repeat for the other back overlay. Cut away the excess stabilizer.

5 Cut overlays along the shoulder, arm curves and sides only, without cutting the rest of the pattern (**FIG. 21**).

6 Stitch the shoulder seams with a ¼" (6 mm) French seam using Madeira thread and size 60 or 70 needle taking a total seam allowance of ½" (1.3 cm).

7 Fold back the facings ¼" (6 mm) then again ¾" (2 cm) as indicated on the pattern. Straight-stitch along the fold edge.

8 Reset your machine with an embroidery needle and Mettler 60 wt cotton or 40 wt rayon thread. Select a satin-stitch scallop design from your machine-stitch library (our scallops are ¾" [2 cm] wide). Place a layer of stabilizer beneath the fabric and follow the neckline of the overlay starting at the center front and stitching to the back fold edge (**FIG. 22**). Repeat for the other side from center front to the back fold edge.

9 Cut away the excess stabilizer and soak the overlay. Once dry, starch and press well. Trim the fabric next to the scallop edge.

10 Set up your machine with a cording foot, size 60 or 70 needle and Madeira thread. Set a zigzag stitch (L=1.0; W= 1.5 or 2.0). Place size 12 pearl cotton in the cording foot

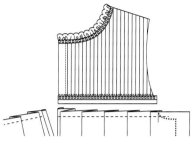

FIGURE 20

FIGURE 21

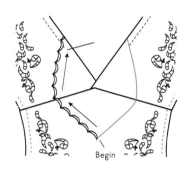

FIGURE 22

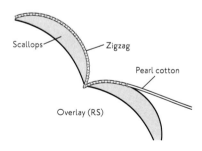

FIGURE 23

and stitch the cord along the outer edge of the satin-stitched scallops (this requires careful pivoting and stitches best with tear-away stabilizer beneath) **(FIG. 23)**.

11 Switch to a regular sewing foot and set your machine for a straight stitch; sew side seams using a ¼" (6 mm) French seam taking a total of ½" (1.3 cm) seam allowance.

12 Slightly gather lace edging and zigzag (L=1.0; W= 1.5 or 2.0) the lace heading to the lower scalloped line of the overlay block **(FIG. 24)**. Trim the fabric under the lace ½" (1.3 cm) from the stitching line and press the excess back away from the lace. Clip the points so that the fabric will lie flat. Zigzag again along the header of lace and trim the excess fabric close to the stitching on the wrong side **(FIG. 25)**.

13 Mark and stitch three buttonholes on the right side back facing. Mark and stitch buttons on the left side. Set the overlay aside.

Zigzag lace to scallop line

FIGURE 24

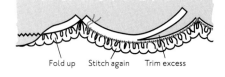

(WS) Lower overlay

Fold up   Stitch again   Trim excess

FIGURE 25

Sleeves

1. The flowers embroidered on the sleeve were taken from design mp2008. Set up your machine with an embroidery needle and thread. On a scrap of fabric, stitch out just the flowers from this motif and mark the center of the fabric while in the hoop. Use this as a template to plan and mark placement of the flowers on the sleeves. Space the flower sets out evenly and rotate as if the sleeve is sprinkled with flowers.

2. Hoop the section of the sleeve to be embroidered with two layers of stabilizer; stitch out two flowers from mp2008. Rehoop another section, align as marked and stitch two more flowers. Continue until the sleeves are complete. Cut out the sleeves.

3. The cuffs should have been pintucked previously. Stitch entredeux on each side of the cuff; roll and whip as instructed previously. Press the seams toward the cuff and straight-stitch or zigzag to secure the seams.

4. Trim the seam tape from one side of the cuff. Gather the lace edging with a 2-to-1 ratio and butt the lace heading to the edge of the trimmed entredeux and join with a zigzag stitch (**FIG. 26**).

5. Gather the lower edge of the sleeve to fit the remaining side of the cuff with the entredeux seam tape. Pin the cuff to the gathered sleeve with the right sides together and stitch in the ditch of the entredeux. Trim the seam to ⅛" (3 mm) and roll and whip with a zigzag. Press the seam away from the cuff and straight-stitch or zigzag from the right side to secure the seam (**FIG. 27**).

6. Stitch the sleeve seam with a rolled-and-whipped finish, or a French seam (taking a total of ½" [1.3 cm] seam allowance).

7. Stitch the yoke front to the skirt front with right sides together and the edge of the entredeux seam to the top edge of the pleated skirt. Stitch in the ditch of the entredeux, trim the seam and roll and whip with a zigzag.

8. Align the back yokes to the back skirt right sides together with the fold of the yoke facing aligned with the fold of the skirt placket. Stitch in the ditch of the entredeux, trim the seam and roll and whip.

9. Press all the seams away from the entredeux. To secure the seams away from the entredeux, straight-stitch or zigzag along the edge of the entredeux on top of the seam from the right side.

10. Mark and stitch three buttonholes on the right side back facing. Mark and stitch buttons on the left side.

11. Place the overlay on the pintucked yoke and align the arm curves and the side seams. Baste the armholes together (**FIG. 28**).

12. Pin entredeux to the armhole with the right sides together beginning and ending at the side seam underarm (**FIG. 29**). Stitch in the ditch of the entredeux, trim the seam to ⅛" (3 mm) and roll and whip the seam with a zigzag. Press the seam back away from the entredeux. To secure the seam, straight-stitch or zigzag.

13. Run two rows of gathering stitches in the sleeve cap and gather the sleeve to fit the armhole along the entredeux seam tape. Stitch in the ditch of the entredeux, trim the seam to ⅛" (3 mm) and roll and whip the seam with a zigzag. Press the seam back away from the entredeux. To secure the seam, straight-stitch or zigzag.

14. Fold and press up the hem ¼" (6 mm), then 1½" (3.8 cm) to the inside of the dress. Hand blind-stitch to secure.

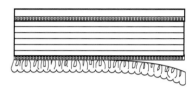

FIGURE 26

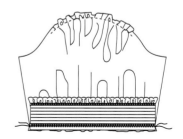

FIGURE 27

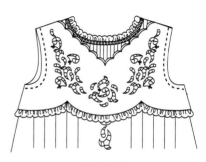

FIGURE 28

FIGURE 29

Elizabeth's Red Dress

BY AMELIA JOHANSON

KNOWING WE WERE PLANNING TO MAKE A VARIATION of Prince William's red and white smocked shirt and shorts, we couldn't resist buying a little red silk dress with white detailing when we saw it at an antiques store for $10. After carefully picking out the seams (it had been hand-constructed), we worked up this adorable pattern. What a sweet pairing it makes with William's suit for a brother/sister ensemble.

What You'll Need...

PATTERN
(available on the CD-rom)

"Elizabeth's Red Dress" (sizes 3 and 4)

FABRIC
(size chart, layout guide, and yardage requirements provided on the CD-rom)

Red fabric (silk/cotton Elegance shown from Martha Pullen Company)

⅛ yd (11.5 cm) of white/cream fabric

TRIM
Six buttons (three decorative for front, three for back)

SUPPLIES
⅛ yd (11.5 cm) of Dreamweave interfacing

Aleene's Original Tacky Glue glue stick

Sewing thread to match fabric and trim

Edge/joining foot for sewing machine

Pilot Fixion iron-away marking pen

FINISHED GARMENT

Size 3
9⅜" (23.7 cm) across front yoke
10" (25.5 cm) across back yoke
19½" (49.5 cm) long (center back to finished hem)

Size 4
10⅛" (25.7 cm) across front yoke
10⅝" (26.7 cm)
20½" (52 cm) long (center back to finished hem)

What to Cut...

FROM THE MAIN FABRIC (RED)

Two front yokes (one lining)

Two back yokes on fold

Four sleeves (two are lining)

One front skirt on fold

One back skirt on fold

11" × ¾" (28 × 2 cm) piece from selvage

FROM CONTRAST FABRIC (WHITE/CREAM)

Four collars

2¼" × 24" (5.5 × 61 cm) bias piece to finish neck edge

FROM INTERFACING

Two collars

How to Make It...

Once all pieces are cut out, use an iron-away marking pen to mark all tuck lines and dots, which will be used to line up pieces during construction. Seam allowances are ⅝" (1.5 cm) for this pattern.

1 Starting from one side of your front skirt piece, fold in the pleats as indicated on the pattern and press (**FIG. 1**). Fold back the pleats, and lightly glue-baste just under the area where the pleats come together for about 4" (10 cm). Fold the pleats back to meet and press to set the glue.

2 Using an edge/joining foot and a right needle position of 1.8 (about ¹⁄₁₆" [2 mm]) from pleat fold, stitch down the right pleat for 4" (10 cm), pivot, stitch across two stitches and stitch back up the left pleat while the guide blade rides in between the pleats (**FIG. 2**).

3 Repeat for all the pleats on the front skirt and back skirt. Stay-stitch across the tops of the skirt to secure the pleats. Clip to the stay-stitching line at the "V" to the dot (**FIG. 3**).

4 Stay-stitch the bottom edge of the dress front yoke along the stitching line. Clip to the dot at the center point of the yoke to mark the center (**FIG. 4**).

5 Line up yoke center to the skirt center with right sides together

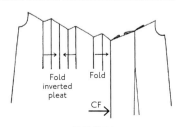

Fold inverted pleat

Fold

CF

FIGURE 1

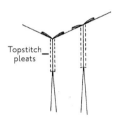

Topstitch pleats

FIGURE 2

and pin half of the top edge. Stitch from the center out (**FIG. 5**). Clip the seam at the center to pivot and repeat to attach the other side of the yoke. Set front aside to prepare back.

6 Create a 5" (12.5 cm) back placket; refer to the Placket instructions in the Techniques section on page 124 if needed.

7 Fold the back yoke piece right sides together and sandwich the right back skirt in between, aligning the fold of the yoke to the edge of the placket opening, placing raw edges even. Stitch across catching all three layers (**FIG. 6**). Flip the yoke up. Repeat for the left side of the back skirt, but make sure the placket edge is folded to the back side. Topstitch across the back yokes just beyond the seam if desired.

8 Join the front yoke to the back yokes at the shoulder seams, keeping the back lining out of the way. Press the seam open. Press up the seam allowance on the yoke front lining piece at the bottom. Join to the back lining pieces right sides together at the shoulders (**FIG. 7**). Press the seams open. Flip the dress right side out; press. Pin the folded-under front yoke lining edge to the yoke front seam allowance. Stay-stitch through both layers around the neckline and armscyes making sure the layers are smooth and aligned properly (**FIG. 8**).

9 Slipstitch to secure the lining to the yoke along the seamline, or remove the pins and glue-baste the lining a scant 1/16" (1 mm) beyond the seam. On the right side, topstitch the yoke a scant 1/8" (3 mm) from the seam using the edge/joining foot; this will catch the lining on the inside (**FIG. 9**).

10 Apply interfacing to the collar pieces. Right sides together, stitch around the collar and collar lining pieces, leaving the neck edge open. Trim the seam allowance to 1/4" (6 mm), clip curves and across the corners (**FIG. 10**). Turn the collar right side out, carefully push out the corners. Press. Stay-stitch around the neck securing the collar and lining together.

11 Pin the collar to the neck edge so that the front edges touch on the seam allowance line at the center front of the yoke. This will make the seam allowance of the collars overlap above the seamline. Stitch the collar to the neckline (**FIG. 11**).

12 Finish the neck edge with a bias binding; refer to the Bias Binding instructions in the Techniques section on page 124 if needed.

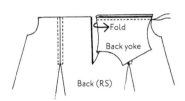

FIGURE 6

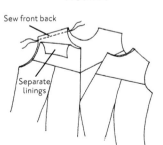

FIGURE 7

FIGURE 8

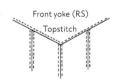

FIGURE 9

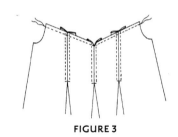

FIGURE 3

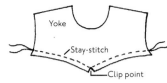

FIGURE 4

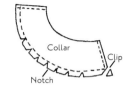

FIGURE 10

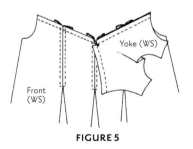

FIGURE 5

FIGURE 11

13 Place a sleeve and lining piece right sides together and stitch across the bottom. Trim the seam to ¼" (6 mm) and clip along the slight curve **(FIG. 12)**. Turn the sleeve to the right side and press along the fold. Repeat for remaining sleeve. Separate the sleeve and lining. Pin the sleeve seams with the right sides together (sleeve to sleeve and lining to lining) matching the bottom seam and stitch **(FIG 13)**. Press the seam open. Fold the sleeve and lining back together. Baste the top edge together to treat the layers as one. Sew the gathering stitching in the sleeve cap. Set the sleeve aside to sew the dress sides seams.

14 Stitch up the sides of the dress aligning the lower edges and underarm. Finish the seam with a zigzag or serger.

15 Gather the sleeve to fit the armscye and stitch the sleeve to the dress with right sides together. Trim the seam and finish the raw edges **(FIG. 14)**.

16 Apply three decorative buttons to the center of the front yoke; refer to photo for placement.

17 Apply three buttonholes and buttons to the back yoke.

18 Turn up the hem ½" (1.3 cm) around the skirt and press. Using the edge/joining foot, topstitch just inside the fold edge a scant ⅛" (3 mm). Carefully trim away the fabric allowance on the inside of the skirt hem right next to the topstitching line making sure not to cut the dress or clip the stitching **(FIG. 15)**. Turn back less than a ¼" (6 mm) and press so you have no pleats or puckers and topstitch again, using the edge/joining foot **(FIG. 16)**. This topstitched hem works best on the pleated silk dress as a slipstitch is easily seen, and a deep hem is not advisable on this slightly flared skirt.

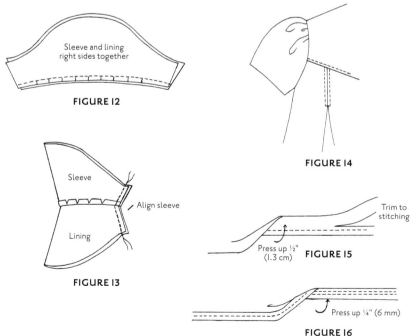

Sleeve and lining right sides together

FIGURE 12

FIGURE 14

Sleeve

Lining

Align sleeve

FIGURE 13

Press up ½" (1.3 cm)

Trim to stitching

FIGURE 15

Press up ¼" (6 mm)

FIGURE 16

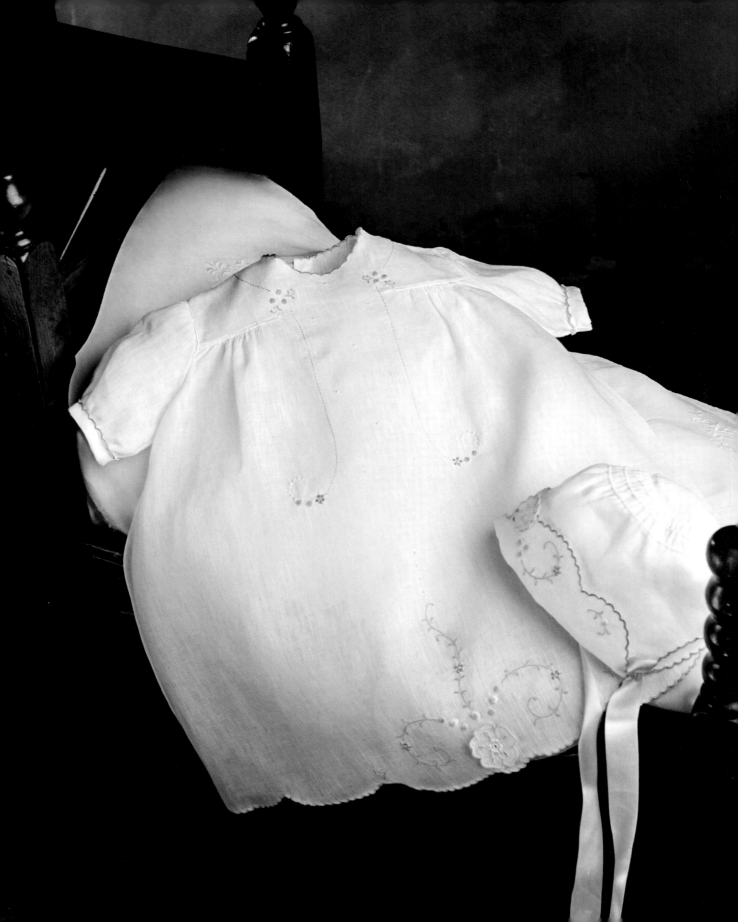

Princess Charlotte Baby Dress & Bonnet

BY WENDY POCHE SCHOEN

WHAT BETTER WAY TO PREPARE FOR A BABY'S ARRIVAL than by creating this exquisite little dress and matching bonnet. Made of imported linen, Wendy's designs are beautifully hand-embroidered with bullion roses and swirling stems. Little eyelets and granitos are scattered about, and a pretty detached appliqué dogwood flower is positioned front and center on the skirt and bonnet. Swirling trails of stem stitch accentuate the delicate nature of the design. Edges are finshed in tiny buttonhole scalloping. Worked entirely with Coton á Broder (broder cotton) in pastel hues, the vintage-look dress design features a T-style yoke and three-quarter-length sleeves gathered and edged with scalloped sleeve bands.

What You'll Need...

PATTERNS
(available on the CD-rom)

"Princess Charlotte Dress and Bonnet" (6 mos. size only)

Dogwood flower template

Hand-embroidery design

FABRIC
(layout guides provided on the CD-rom)

2 yd (1.8 m) of fine white linen

¼ yd (23 cm) of white cotton organza

⅓ yd (30.5 cm) of pink cotton organza

TRIM

1¼ yd (1.2 m) of white Swiss entredeux

5 yd (457.5 cm) of light blue 1" (2.5 cm) wide silk satin ribbon

2 yd (1.8 m) of light blue ⅝" (1.5 cm) wide silk satin ribbon

Four ¼" (6 mm) wide mother-of-pearl buttons

THREAD

DMC Coton á Broder #25

Skein Blanc

Skein Green #472

Skein Yellow #745

Skein Pink #776

Skein Pink #819

Two Skeins Blue #3325

Basting thread

SUPPLIES

Fine-point blue wash-away marking pen *or* #2 lead pencil

6" (15 cm) hands-free hoop *or* 4" (10 cm) Susan Bates hoop

Magnification and light

Embroidery needles

#8 crewel

#8 sharps

#10 sharps

Embroidery scissors

Shears

Clear plastic ruler

Measuring tape

Thimble and finger shield

Glass-head pins

Clover tapered awl

Pinning board and pins

What to Cut...

Before starting, section off the white linen into individual blocks for each pattern piece. (Refer to the layout guide on the CD-rom before proceeding.)

FROM LINEN

23" (L) × 28" (W) (58.5 × 71 cm) block for the dress front

20" (L) × 30" (W) (51 × 76 cm) block for the dress back

12" (L) × 7½" (W) (30.5 × 19 cm) block for the yoke

12" (L) × 20" (W) (30.5 × 51 cm) block for the bonnet

8" (20.5 cm) square for sleeve bands

Two sleeves

FROM PINK ORGANZA

Two 12" (30.5 cm) squares for flower appliqué (one for dress, one for bonnet)

FROM WHITE ORGANZA

8" (30.5 cm) square for the sleeve band interlining

12" (L) × 20" (W) (30.5 × 51 cm) block for the bonnet

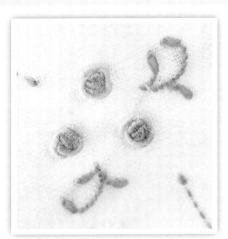

How to Make It...

Preparation

1 Spritz with water and then spray starch and iron the fabric blocks dry. Repeat the process, if necessary.

2 Pin the fabric blocks over their respective pattern pieces and transfer the embroidery designs with a blue wash-away marking pen. (See Using the Pinning Board sidebar.)

Embroidery

Most of the embroidery is worked without an embroidery hoop, but eyelet and stem stitch look better when worked with a hoop. Work these stitches before proceeding to the other stitches. Refer to the Techniques section on page 124 for specific embroidery-stitch instructions.

Using a Pinning Board

Refer to **FIG. 1** for all steps.

1 Place the embroidery template face up and centered on a pinning board. Carefully position and secure the prepared fabric block over the design, right side up. Start pinning by the first pin at the center top edge. Smooth the fabric down tightly and place a pin at the center lower edge.

2 Working out about 1½" (3.8 cm), place another pin and repeat the smoothing process to apply the pin at the lower edge. Continue until the entire top and bottom edges of the fabric are pinned in place and then repeat for the sides.

3 Transfer the embroidery design onto the fabric block using a #2 lead pencil or a fine-point wash-away marking pen. Make certain the design is centered and on grain.

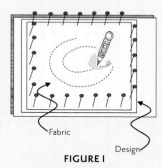

Fabric

Design

FIGURE 1

Applying an Embroidery Hoop

Refer to **FIGS. 2 AND 3** for all steps.

1 Notice that there is an inner hoop with a rim, or lip, on one edge on the Susan Bates hoop. Place the inner hoop down onto the table with the rim side up.

2 Place the fabric, right side up with the embroidery design centered within the hoop.

3 Loosen the tension of the screw on the outer hoop and place it over the inner hoop, sandwiching the fabric between. Push the outer hoop over the inner hoop until it is flush with the table.

4 Pick up the hoop, giving it one more push until the inner hoop pops over the outer hoop. Grabbing all the fabric into your non-stitching hand, smooth the fabric. Tighten the screw slightly. Continue smoothing the fabric as you complete the tightening.

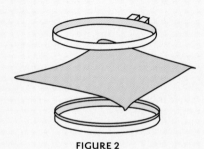

FIGURE 2

FIGURE 3

Detached Appliqué

1 Transfer the flower template onto the starched square of pink organza (**FIG. 4**).

2 Complete the buttonhole stitching around the edges of the flower and the teardrop eyelets (**FIG. 5**).

3 Cut out the appliqué close to the edges (**FIG. 6**).

4 Complete all the embroidery on the gown, except the circle of dots (granitos) at the center front lower edge of the dress. (This marks the center of the flower to attach the appliqué.)

5 Position the detached appliqué over the circle of dots on the gown. Pin or baste in place.

6 Complete the circle of dots embroidery (granitos) through the appliqué and dress fabric; cut out all the pattern pieces making sure hems and armholes align.

FIGURE 4

FIGURE 5

FIGURE 6

Buttonhole Edge

1 Before proceeding with the buttonhole edging on the neck, turn the back yoke facings back along the folding line **(FIG. 7)**. Turn the raw edge under ¼" (6 mm) and baste in place; press well.

2 Complete the buttonhole edge around the neck edge, stitching through all layers of the facing.

Dress Construction

All seams are ⅜" (I cm).

1 Machine stay-stitch along the seams of the yoke slashes on the dress front (L=2.0). Cut the slit between the stitches **(FIG. 8)**.

2 Stitch three gathering rows along the lower edge of the slit, placing the first row ⅛" (3 mm) from the edge and each ⅛" (3 mm) thereafter. Attach entredeux to the upper edges with right sides together, stitching to the large dot indicated on the pattern **(FIG. 9)**. Refer to French sewing in the Techniques section on page 124 if necessary.

3 Pull in the gathers on the lower edge to fit the entredeux. Pin in place with the right sides together, distributing gathers evenly **(FIG. 10)**.

4 Repeat for the other side.

5 Work a 5" (12.5 cm) continuous lap placket at the upper back center of the skirt. Refer to Placket in the Techniques section, if necessary.

6 Stitch three gathering rows along the back skirt edges placing the first stitching line ⅛" (3 mm) from the edge, and having them ⅛" (3 mm) apart (L=2.4) **(FIG. 11)**.

7 Attach entredeux to the back yoke bottom edges **(FIG. 12)**. Roll and whip the raw edges together.

8 Pull in the gathers so they are even with the yoke's lower edge. Distribute the gathers evenly, and pin them to the entredeux with the right sides together. Stitch very close to the entredeux, taking in ¼" (6 mm) seams **(FIG. 13)**. Roll and whip the raw edges together.

9 French seam the shoulders together using a very narrow seam **(FIG. 14)**. Press the seams to the back; refer to French Seam in the Techniques section on page 124 if necessary.

10 Complete the hem embroidery and cut away the excess fabric from below the scallops on the hem **(FIG. 15)**.

11 French seam the gown front to back at the sides using a very narrow seam, making certain the scallops meet at the sides **(FIG. 16)**.

12 Stitch the underarm tucks along the stitching line as indicated on the pattern **(FIG. 17)**. Fold the seam even with the stitches, opening the tuck out. Press and baste in place **(FIG. 18)**.

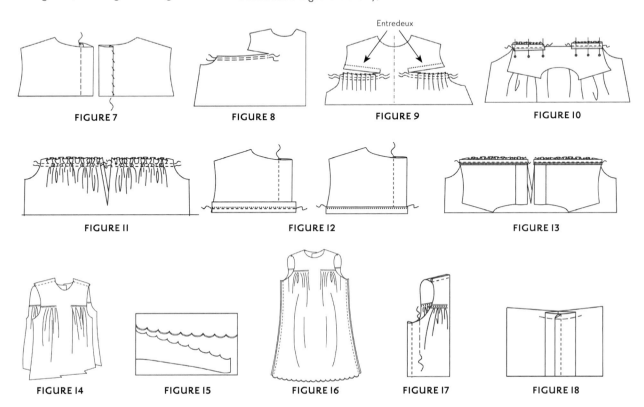

FIGURE 7   FIGURE 8   FIGURE 9   FIGURE 10

FIGURE 11   FIGURE 12   FIGURE 13

FIGURE 14   FIGURE 15   FIGURE 16   FIGURE 17   FIGURE 18

Sleeves

1 Trace the sleeve cuff template onto the linen block. To stabilize, baste white organdy to the wrong side of the cuff. These pieces will be treated as one fabric.

2 Stitch a running stitch along the outer scallop edge through all fabric layers with one strand of blue broder floss.

3 Work a close buttonhole stitch along the scallops **(FIG. 19)**. Cut away the excess fabric from the scallops.

4 With right sides together, sew the ends of the cuffs together to form a circle **(FIG. 20)**. Overcast the raw edges. Press the seams open.

5 Ease-stitch three rows of gathering stitches along the lower and upper edges of the sleeve beginning ⅛" (3 mm) from the edge and placing each row ⅛" (3 mm) apart (L=2.5) **(FIG. 21)**.

6 French seam the sleeve with right sides together and edges even. Press the seam to the back.

7 Pull in the gathers at the lower edge to fit the cuff **(FIG. 22)**. Position the right side of the cuff to the wrong side of the sleeve. Stitch, taking in ¼" (6 mm) seams **(FIG. 23)**. Overcast the raw edges. Press the cuff and seam down **(FIG. 24)**. Turn the sleeve right side out; press. Turn the cuff to the right side, folding along the seamline. Press in place **(FIG. 25)**.

8 Attach entredeux to the armhole opening on the yoke. Trim, then roll and whip the raw edges. Ease in the gathers of the sleeve to fit the armhole opening **(FIG. 26)**. Pin the sleeve to the armhole opening, aligning the seams. Baste in place. Stitch the sleeve to the entredeux. Roll and whip the raw edges. Repeat for the other sleeve.

Finishing

1 Sew two buttons to the left back yoke **(FIG. 27)**.

2 Make buttonholes in the right back yoke to match the buttons.

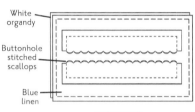

White organdy
Buttonhole stitched scallops
Blue linen

FIGURE 19

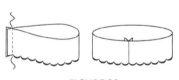

FIGURE 20

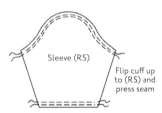

Sleeve (RS)
Flip cuff up to (RS) and press seam

FIGURE 21

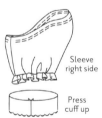

Sleeve right side
Press cuff up

FIGURE 22

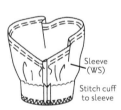

Sleeve (WS)
Stitch cuff to sleeve

FIGURE 23

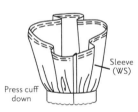

Sleeve (WS)
Press cuff down

FIGURE 24

FIGURE 25

FIGURE 26

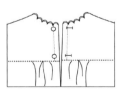

FIGURE 27

Bonnet

1 Transfer the embroidery template onto the linen bonnet block.

2 Pin the organdy block to the wrong side of the linen (**FIG. 28**). On the back edges, turn the organdy under along the seamlines, then baste the two fabrics together all around (**FIG. 29**). These pieces will be treated as one fabric.

3 From the linen side, work the buttonhole scallop edge along the front edge from the foldline to the foldline. This flap will be turned back.

4 From the organdy side, work the buttonhole edge along the sides from the foldline to the foldline. This part of the bonnet will be on the outside, so the scallops are worked on the organdy side.

5 Complete the embroidery entirely and cut out the pattern pieces, trimming very close to the scalloped edges. NOTE: *The embroidery is worked on the linen side, then the linen is turned back to form the brim. For flower appliqué refer to dress embroidery for instructions.*

Bonnet Assembly

1 Stitch three rows of gathering along the back edge of the bonnet on the lines indicated (L=2.5) (**FIG. 30**).

2 Sew cording along the three marked lines, inserting the cord between the lining and fabric. With a twin needle, stitch through both layers holding the cording between the two needles (L=2.0) (**FIG. 31**).

3 French seam the back together aligning the notches and edges, and keeping the cording away from the stitching (**FIG. 32**). Press the seam to one side.

4 Spray starch and iron a 9" (23 cm) length of entredeux. Trim one batiste edge to ¼" (6 mm).

5 On the crown, pin the entredeux to the edges, right sides together, clipping as necessary to form a circle. Stitch in place (**FIG. 33**).

6 Pull in the gathers on the bonnet back edge with right sides together and then pin the crown in place, adjusting the gathers evenly (**FIG. 34**).

7 Draw up the cords to form ruching on the back, adjusting the gathers as necessary. Bring the cords to the inside with a large-eyed needle, and then tie into bows.

8 Hand-stitch the organdy edges together in back.

9 Sew ribbon ties to the bonnet sides on the inside.

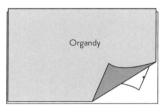

Organdy

FIGURE 28

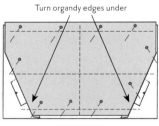

Turn organdy edges under

FIGURE 29

FIGURE 30

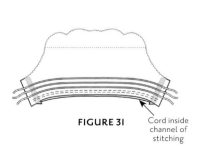

FIGURE 31

Cord inside channel of stitching

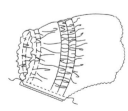

FIGURE 32

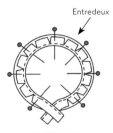

Entredeux

FIGURE 33

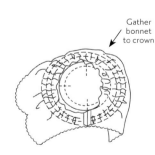

Gather bonnet to crown

FIGURE 34

SEWING FOR A
Little
Prince

THERE IS SUCH A SMALL WINDOW of opportunity to dress your little boy in the finery you pour so much love into, so don't let those precious years pass you by. Bubble suits are baby-boy staples. Inspired by the sailor suit that's remained in favor since Queen Victoria had one made for her son Prince Albert Edward, we drafted a special front-button Ascot Collar to fit one of our favorite bubble-suit patterns. With the addition of bias trim, the unique take on a sailor collar becomes an instant classic. We included two shorts designs, classic button-on and basic pull-on styles. Either is interchangeable with three different shirts. As a child, Prince William was frequently photographed wearing English smocking, and Laurie Anderson worked up a reproduction of one of his shirts with an original smocking plate you can use to accent the button-front design. Our pleated-front Belle Heir Shirt is an antique reproduction designed with a V-shaped yoke and the added interest of piping set into every tuck. The short sleeve has a little boy vibe, but pair the sleeveless option with a button-on skirt (pattern not included), and suddenly the ensemble has little girl written all over it. Our third shirt is the Little Lad tunic topper, also a reproduction, and it has clean, asymmetrical lines and braided trim for a regal look that suits every little prince.

Prince William's Suit

BY LAURIE ANDERSON

Britain's Prince William waves as he leaves St. Mary's Hospital in Paddington, London, after visiting his mother, Princess Diana, and her new baby son, September 16, 1984. (AP Photo)

On SEPTEMBER 16, 1984, little Prince William, dressed in an English smocked shirt with matching red shorts was introduced to his new little brother, Harry (Henry Charles Albert David). Photos of William clutching his nanny's hand as he left St. Mary's Hospital in London circulated around the world. Laurie Anderson based this little boy's suit on that precious moment. While she reproduced her vision in red and white, true to the original look and a perfect paring for the Elizabeth's Red Dress on page 43, the outfit could be made in any color combination to suit your tastes.

What You'll Need...

PATTERN
(available on the CD-rom)

"Prince William's Shirt" (sizes 1 to 4), adapted to front smocking

"William's Pull-on Shorts" (sizes 1 to 4)

Royal Diamond Chevron smocking design (page 59)

FABRIC
(size chart, layout guide, and yardage requirements provided on the CD-rom)

White batiste (60" wide [152.5 cm])

Red cotton broadcloth for lined pull-on shorts (add ½ yd [46 cm] extra for matching piping for shirt, or purchase ready-made piping to match).

SUPPLIES
Five ⅜" (1 cm) shirt buttons

Two ½" (1.3 cm) buttons

6"–8" (15–20.5 cm) of 1" (2.5 cm) wide elastic

Mini piping cord or purchased white mini piping

Quilting thread for pleater

Basting glue stick

Pleater

DMC Cotton Embroidery Floss in color to match color of broadcloth

#817 red shown

⅛ yd (11.5 cm) of lightweight interfacing (for waistband)

Sewing thread to match fabrics

Machine feet:

Edge/joining

Grooved

What to Cut...

FROM BATISTE (WHITE)
Two 30" × 4" (76 × 10 cm) strips for smocking insert

Two sleeves

Four collars (two are lining)

Two 6" × 10" (15 × 25.5 cm) blocks for shirt yokes

Two 12" × 10" (30.5 × 25.5 cm) blocks for lower shirt pieces

One back shirt on fold

1½" × 24" (3.8 × 61 cm) bias strip for self-piping, or purchase ready-made white cotton piping

19" × 1" (48.5 × 2.5 cm) bias band for the neck facing

FROM BROADCLOTH (RED)
Four shorts fronts (two are for lining)

Four shorts backs (two are for lining)

Front waistband

1½" × 36" (3.8 × 91.5 cm) bias strip for self-piping on shirt, or purchase ready-made piping to match

FROM INTERFACING
Front waistband

How to Make It...

Smocked Inserts

1 Cut 60" × 4" (152.5 × 10 cm) strip of batiste into two 30" × 4" (76 × 10 cm) strips. Pleat each piece with seven rows.

2 After pleating, block the insert to the correct width for each side. To determine this width, measure across the shirt front pattern piece just below the lower armscye.

3 Remove the guide threads from 1⅝" (4.13 cm) on the inside edge of the left insert and tie off (this flat section will be sewn in with the front closure). Likewise, remove the guide threads 1¼" (6 mm) from the inside edge of the right insert. Leave 1" (2.5 cm) flat on the opposite ends on both inserts to accommodate the armscye **(FIG. 1)**. Your pleated block with flat sections on each side should measure the width determined by the width of the shirt pattern in Step 2.

4 Smock each insert. (Refer to directions for Royal Diamond Chevrons).

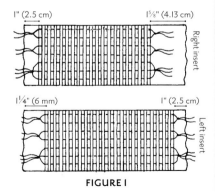

1" (2.5 cm)　　　　1⅝" (4.13 cm)

Right insert

1¼" (6 mm)　　　　1" (2.5 cm)

Left insert

FIGURE 1

Royal Diamond Chevron Smocking

BY LAURIE ANDERSON

Design as shown was smocked with three strands of DMC #817 red six-strand embroidery floss.

1 Pleat seven rows. Mark center pleat with a wash-away marking pen. Rows 1 and 7 are holding rows and will not be smocked. Block 102 pleats for each insert. (Refer to Royal Diamond Chevrons smocking graph below.)

2 For the upper border, start at the center two pleats and cable across Row 1, beginning with an up cable. Invert your work and complete the other side of the cable row.

3 On Row 1 under the first down cable, work a three-cable combination starting with an up cable, step down to Row 1½, and trellis-stitch over just one pleat, down cable one. Step back up to Row 1 and over just one pleat beginning on the same pleat continue the pattern across the row. Smock carefully and remember to trellis up and down on the same pleat as the previous cable.

4 Start the bottom border at the center two pleats on Row 5 and work a mirror image of the upper border between Rows 5 and 5½.

5 Between Rows 2 and 2½ and Rows 3 and 3½, work a half-step wave across the row, beginning with a down cable.

6 Mirror image a half-step wave between Rows 2½ and 3 and 3½ and 4.

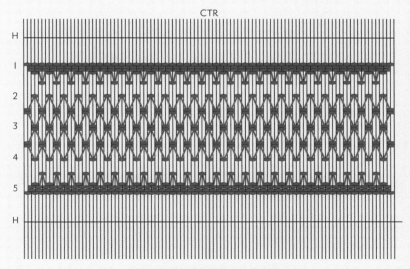

CTR

**ROYAL DIAMOND CHEVRONS
SMOCKING GRAPH**

5 Create white self-piping with mini cord and the bias strip of batiste; refer to Piping in the Techniques section on page 124 or use premade mini piping. Align the strip of piping a scant ¼" (6 mm) above the upper smocked border using a ruler's edge to ensure the piping is aligned with the cable row. Glue-baste the piping to the insert. Using a grooved foot, place the piping in the groove and stitch just inside the stitching line of the piping to secure it to the insert. Repeat for the lower edge of this insert and for the upper and lower edges of the second insert.

Prepping the Shirt Pattern for Smocked Inserts

1 Stitch the 10" (25.5 cm) long edge of the 6" × 10" (15 × 25.5 cm) yoke block to the upper piped edge of each smocked insert **(FIG. 2)**. The block measurements are given to accommodate the largest shirt size, so trim any excess fabric away on the sides for the smaller sizes.

2 The lower part of the featured shirt is plain. If you would prefer, you can pleat or tuck a larger block of fabric to apply to the lower edge of the insert. NOTE: *Make sure the pleats are mirror image on each side and press before joining the block to the inserts.*

3 Once the blocks are stitched to the inserts, pin the shirt front pattern pieces to the fabric, lining up the lower piped edge of the smocked insert with the lower armscye. The pattern calls for a folded front facing, but a separately stitched placket is required for the left (overlapping) side on this design. The right side will remain a folded facing. You will need 1¾" (4.5 cm) flat fabric from the center front line on the right side and 1⅛" (3 cm) from the center front line on the left side **(FIG. 3)**. Cut out, making certain that the shirt fronts line up on either side so the smocking will meet horizontally at the center.

4 Fold back the right shirt edge ¼" (6 mm), and again 1" (2.5 cm). Press and stitch to complete the button side of the front closure.

5 Press under ¼" (6 mm) to the wrong side along the longest edge of the left front placket piece. With the right side of strip to the wrong side of shirt front, raw edges together, stitch a ⅝" (1.5 cm) seam. Trim the seam to ¼" (6 mm). Press the placket to the front, enclosing the seam. Topstitch on both sides of the placket to complete the buttonhole side of the front closure **(FIG. 4)**.

6 Seams from this point on are ¼" (6 mm).

Sleeves

1 Create red self-piping with mini cord and the bias strip of broadcloth; refer to Piping in the Techniques section on page 124, or use premade mini piping. Measure the bottom of the sleeve and cut two piping pieces that width. Set the remaining piping aside for the collar.

2 Trim the piping seam allowance to ¼" (6 mm). On the bottom edge of each sleeve, fold ¼" (6 mm) up to the right side and press in place. Place piping along the fold of the sleeve and glue-baste or stitch it to the wrong side **(FIG. 5)**.

3 Turn the raw edges to the right side with the piping on the bottom edge **(FIG. 6)**. Press seam in place.

4 Fold the cuff to the right side on the foldline **(FIG. 7)**. Stitch the cuff in place by stitching in the ditch where the piping was attached.

5 Repeat for the other sleeve. Set aside.

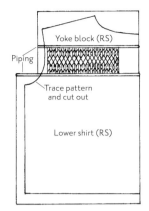

FIGURE 2

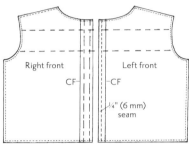

FIGURE 3

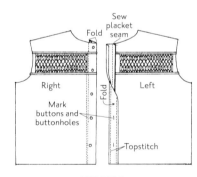

FIGURE 4

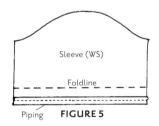

FIGURE 5

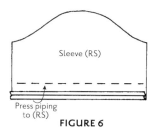

Sleeve (RS)

Press piping
to (RS)

FIGURE 6

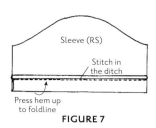

Sleeve (RS)

Stitch in
the ditch

Press hem up
to foldline

FIGURE 7

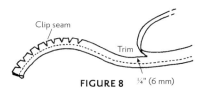

Clip seam

Trim

FIGURE 8 ¼" (6 mm)

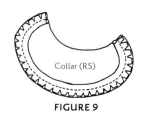

Collar (RS)

FIGURE 9

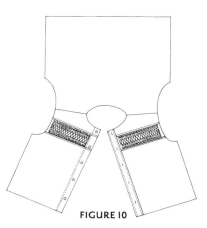

FIGURE 10

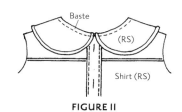

Baste

(RS)

Shirt (RS)

FIGURE 11

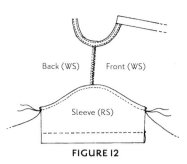

Back (WS) Front (WS)

Sleeve (RS)

FIGURE 12

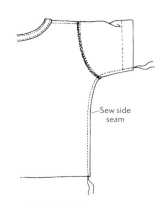

Sew side
seam

FIGURE 13

Collar

1 Trim the piping seam allowance to ¼" (6 mm) and clip every ½" (1.3 cm) to the stitching line so that it will curve around the edge of the collar (**FIG. 8**). With the raw edges even, glue-baste or pin the piping around the outside collar edge. Stitch just inside the piping stitch line to apply (**FIG. 9**).

2 Place the collar lining to the collar with the wrong sides together. Pin. Stitch along the bobbin thread line that secures the piping. Notch the seam around the curves and turn the collar right side out and press. Repeat for the second collar; create a right and left collar. Stay-stitch around the neckline edges to baste the collar and lining layers together.

Constructions

1 With the right sides together, stitch the smocked fronts to the shirt back at the shoulder seams; overcast to finish the seam (**FIG.10**).

2 Place the collar to the neckline with the wrong side of the collar to the right side of shirt. Overlap the front closure so that center front marks align. Pin the collar so that the piping edges will meet at center front (**FIG. 11**). Apply a bias facing using a ¼" (6 mm) seam. Refer to Neck Facing in the Techniques section on page 124.

3 Ease-stitch the cap of the sleeve with two rows of basting stitches. Pin the sleeves around the armscyes and stitch in place (**FIG. 12**). Overcast the seam.

4 Place the sides of the shirt together matching the underarm seam and the bottom of the sleeve Stitch and overcast (**FIG. 13**).

5 Finish the bottom of the shirt with a shirttail hem or serged edge. Space five buttonholes down the

front of the shirt placket. Make buttonholes and sew on the buttons.

Shorts

1 Mark the side dots on the shorts and shorts lining pieces with a wash-away marking pen. This is very important; do not skip this step. Also mark the foldline across the top back.

2 Place one shorts front and one shorts back right sides together at the side seams and stitch from the dot to the bottom (**FIG. 14**); clip at an angle through the seam allowance to the dot. Repeat for the remaining shorts front and back and for the lining pieces.

3 With the right sides of the shorts together (front to front and back to back), stitch the front and back seams (**FIG. 15**). Clip the curves and press the seams open. Repeat for the front and back seams of the lining.

4 Place the lining inside the shorts, right sides together, side seams and crotch seams aligned; pin if needed. Stitch across the bottom of each leg along the seamline; this is closer to a ¾" (2 cm) than the ¼" (6 mm) seam used for the rest of the garment (**FIG. 16**). Turn right side out and press.

5 Pull the shorts lining out from the pants, wrong side out, and align the inseams; pin. The shorts

bottom edges should be joined lining to shorts. Matching the crotch seams, stitch all the way around the inseams in a circle to close (**FIG. 17**). Turn the shorts to the right side by pulling one leg at a time through the open top of the shorts. Press.

6 The shorts and lining are unstitched from the dot to the top. From the wrong side with the right side of the short to the right side of the lining, position your needle where the side seam stitching ends at the dot. Stitch up the shorts front, finishing the side seam (**FIG. 18**). Flip right side out and press. Repeat for the other shorts front. Baste the lining to the shorts across the top edge of the front.

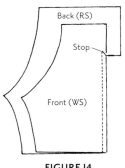

FIGURE 14

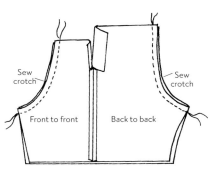

FIGURE 15

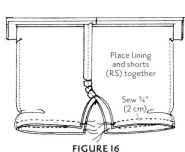

FIGURE 16

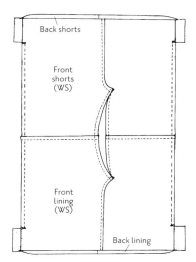

FIGURE 17

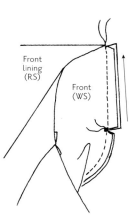

FIGURE 18

7 To finish the side seams on the back, place the shorts extension to the lining extension, right sides together, and from the wrong side, again position your needle where the side seam stitching ends at the dot. This time stitch across the extension to ½" (1.3 cm) from the edge, pivot and stitch to the top of the shorts **(FIG. 19)**. Clip across the corner of the extension; flip to the right side and press. Repeat for the other side of the back. Baste across the back top edge to join both layers together.

8 Stabilize the front waistband by applying lightweight fusible interfacing. Place the waistband to the front edge with the right sides together with shorts sides meeting the seamline of the band at each end **(FIG. 20)**.

9 Press under ¼" (6 mm) to the wrong side on the remaining raw edge of the waistband. Fold the waistband in half along the foldline with right sides together. Stitch the ends, being careful not to catch the pants in the seam and securing well at the bottom edge **(FIG. 21)**. Turn the waistband right side out and to the inside enclosing the seam. Hand whip the fold edge of the band to the inside along the seamline. Sew buttonholes to each end of waistband **(FIG. 22)**.

10 Press under ¼" (6 mm) along the top edges of the shorts back. Fold a casing to the inside along the foldline, to the wrong side, making sure that the top front waistband and the top back are even. Stitch close to both the top and bottom edges of the casing.

11 Cut a piece of elastic to the following measurements:

Sizes 1 and 2
6" (15 cm) and 6½" (16.5 cm)

Sizes 3 and 4
7" (18 cm) and 8" (20.5 cm)

12 Run elastic through the casing using a safety pin on one end of the elastic strip. Pull the elastic through the casing until the opposite end is 1" (2.5 cm) from the casing opening. Secure the elastic end with a neat straight stitch. Remove the safety pin from the front end of the elastic and allow the end to retract into the casing, stopping it 1" (2.5 cm) from the casing opening. Pin to hold and secure this end with a straight stitch **(FIG. 23)**. Close the openings on each end of the casing with a topstitch.

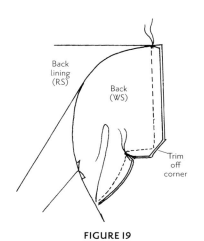

Back lining (RS)

Back (WS)

Trim off corner

FIGURE 19

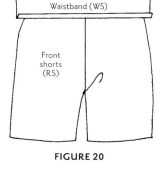

Waistband (WS)

Front shorts (RS)

FIGURE 20

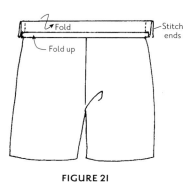

Fold

Fold up

Stitch ends

FIGURE 21

Flip to inside

Sew buttonholes

FIGURE 22

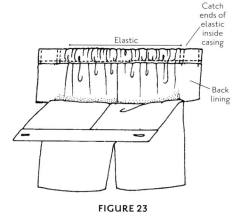

Catch ends of elastic inside casing

Elastic

Back lining

FIGURE 23

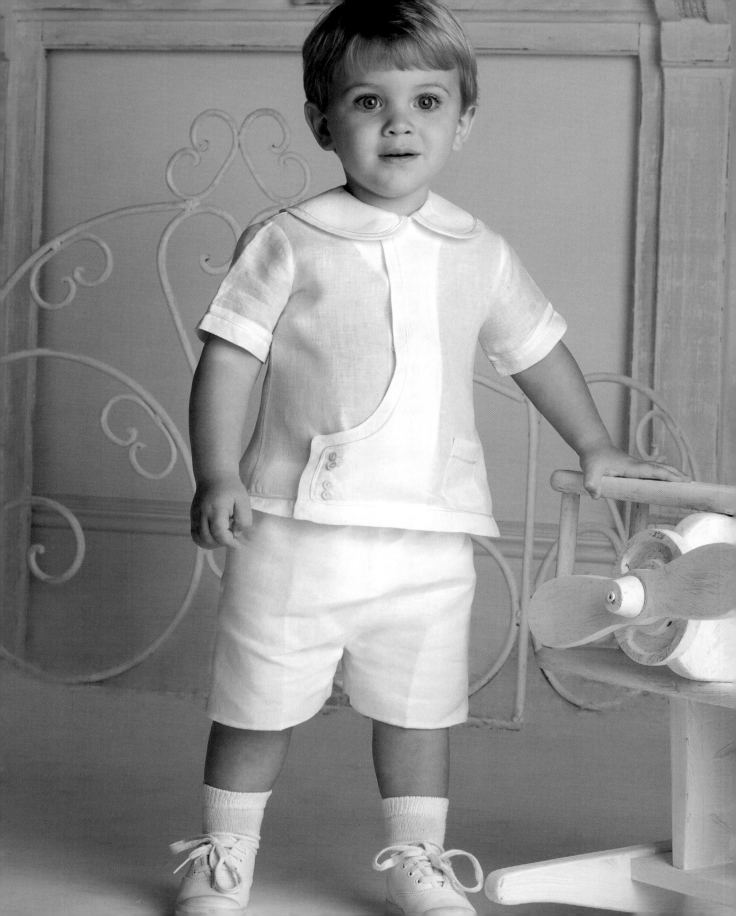

Little Lad Sunday Suit

INSPIRED BY AN ANTIQUE CONSTRUCTED BY HELEN LIVELY

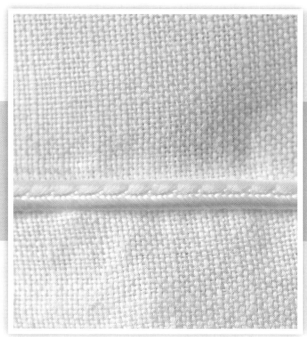 

WHAT WE LIKE ABOUT THIS PATTERN, especially for boys, is that it offers a unique design line that is unmistakably heirloom without being too frilly. The suit is a remake of a vintage piece. The linen top is trimmed with white soutache braid for a clean, white-on-white effect; navy braid would give the suit a sailor look. A contrasting Madeira border, a touch of embroidery, or a different colored fabric for the shorts would be equally appealing.

What You'll Need...

PATTERN

(available on the CD-rom)

"Little Lad Sunday Suit" (sizes 1 to 4)

"William's Pull-on Shorts" (sizes 1 to 4)

FABRIC

(size chart, layout guides, and yardage requirements provided on the CD-rom)

Allow ½ yd (46 cm) extra shirt fabric for self-piping on collar and cuffs, or purchase ready-made piping to match.

White handkerchief linen

White batiste (lining)

TRIM

1½ yd (1.4 m) of white soutache cord

SUPPLIES

Lace-shaping board

Spool of white DMC 50 wt thread

½ yd (46 cm) of piping cord

Four ⅜" (1 cm) buttons

Elastic for shorts

Interfacing (for waistband)

Four plastic sew-on snaps

Roxanne's Glue-Baste-It

Size 70 sharps needle

Size 65 or 70 universal machine needle

Blue wash-away marking pen

Grooved sewing machine foot

What to Cut...

FROM MAIN FABRIC

Right shirt front

Left shirt front

Shirt back

Pocket

Right shirt facing

Left shirt facing

Two sleeves

Two collar blocks (larger than collar)

Two shorts fronts

Two shorts backs

Waistband

1½" (3.8 cm) wide bias strips for self-piping (enough to cover piping around collar and sleeves) or use ready-made piping

FROM LINING FABRIC

One collar block

Two shorts fronts

Two shorts backs

FROM INTERFACING

Waistband

Working with Soutache

1 Soutache braid will shrink. It is very important to preshrink the braid before use, or your garment fabric will pucker around the trim after washing. To shrink soutache, soak it in warm water and allow it to air dry.

2 Shape around the curves by pulling one of the two cords while firmly pushing the rest of the braid away.

3 Place the garment on a lace-shaping board or padded surface and position the cord on the garment, smoothing the braid in place; stab the pin as you would if shaping lace.

4 Apply the basting glue under the line of braid and let it dry.

5 Stitch, using a small stitch (2.0) and fine size 65 or 70 machine needle.

How to Make It...

Preparation

1 Prewash the fabric, dry, starch, and press before cutting out. Preshrink the soutache (see Working with Soutache section).

2 Mark the dots and notches as indicated on the pattern for all pieces. Trace the collar and seamlines onto the two collar blocks. Mark the braid lines ⅜" (1.3 cm) from the seamline.

Instructions

1 Prepare the collars: Place a block of batiste under one linen block and pin in place. Glue-baste the soutache braid on ⅜" (1 cm) guideline and straight-stitch along the center groove of the

braid (FIG. 1). TIP: *Use a grooved foot to secure the braid in the center groove and set the needle position in the center.*

2 Cover the piping cord for the collar and cuffs; refer to Piping in the Techniques section on page 124. Glue-baste the prepared piping to the outer edge of the collar with the raw edge of the piping aligned to the collar cutting line (not the

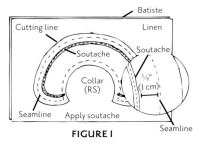

FIGURE 1

seamline). Baste the piping to the collar on the seamline **(FIG. 2)**. TIP: *Use a grooved foot and set the piping in the center groove; adjust the needle position to stitch beside the cording.*

3 Place second block of linen on top so that the right sides are together. Stitch with the batiste side up and use the previous stitching line as a guide. Place the piping hump in the center groove of a grooved machine foot and set the needle position to stitch beside the piping just inside the previous stitch line. Shift the piping to the outer groove of the foot and adjust the needle position to stitch a second line a scant $\frac{1}{8}$" (3 mm) away. Trim close to the second line of stitching **(FIG. 3)**.

4 Notch the $\frac{1}{8}$" (3 mm) seam on the curves and turn the collar right side out. The batiste will serve as the interfacing. Set the collars aside.

5 Prepare the pocket: Fold under and press the top edge of the pockets $\frac{1}{4}$" (6 mm) then $\frac{3}{4}$" (2 cm).

Glue-baste a piece of soutache braid $\frac{5}{8}$" (1.5 cm) from the fold on the right side of the pocket from raw edge to raw edge **(FIG. 4)**. Do not stitch.

6 Fold the top edge of the pocket back on itself to the wrong side so that the braid is sandwiched between. Stitch across the ends of the hem and continue to stay-stitch around the seamline of the pocket curve **(FIG. 5)**. Flip the pocket hem to the inside and press. Notch the curves to the stay-stitching and finger press the edges under. Stitch across the soutache trim from the right side and catch the fold of the hem on the wrong side. Press and starch to set the shape **(FIG. 6)**.

7 Glue-baste the pocket in place on the left front piece and topstitch it to secure **(FIG. 7)**.

8 Prepare the sleeves: Fold and press the bottom edge to the right side of the sleeve along the pattern foldlines. Position and glue the soutache braid $\frac{1}{4}$" (6 mm) down from the top fold edge ($\frac{3}{4}$" [2 cm] from the bottom). Stitch in place catching the hem on

the wrong side **(FIG. 8)**. NOTE: *If your fabric has a distinctive wrong side, fold the hem to the wrong side instead.*

9 Stitch the sleeve seams with a narrow French seam using $\frac{1}{2}$" (1.3 cm) total allowance. Set the sleeves aside.

10 Assemble the top: Stitch the back to the fronts at the shoulder seams and the side seams; use a French seam and press the seams toward the back.

11 Mark a line for the soutache braid beginning at the right front facing edge. This line should be $\frac{5}{8}$" (1.5 cm) above the hemline all around the bottom edge. Continue around the back and work to the right front. Pivot at the bottom right front corner and mark $\frac{5}{8}$" (1.5 cm) from the seamline edge of the right front up to the neckline. Glue-baste the soutache braid to this line and stitch the braid a section of only 6" (15 cm) from the right front edge (do not stitch the remaining braid) **(FIG. 9)**. See the sidebar working with soutache braid on page 66.

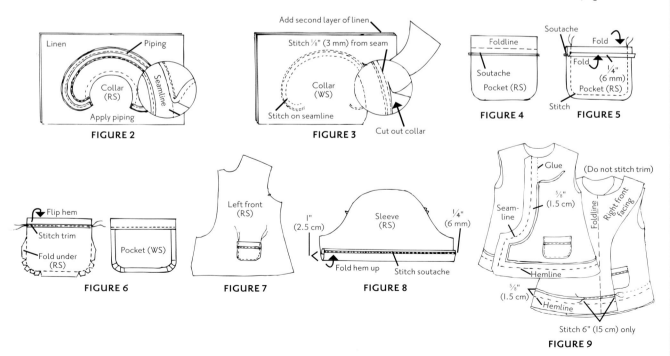

FIGURE 2

FIGURE 3

FIGURE 4   **FIGURE 5**

FIGURE 6   **FIGURE 7**   **FIGURE 8**   **FIGURE 9**

12 Stitch the shoulder seams of the back facing (#6) to the front facings (#5 and #2) (the right facing is attached to the right front). Press the seams open **(FIG. 10)**.

13 Fold a narrow ¼" (6 mm) hem along the outer raw edge of the facings; press and stitch to finish the raw edge.

14 Apply the collar: Pin the prepared collar to the neckline matching the front edges of the collars to the center front dots indicated on the pattern. Fold the right front facing to the right side on the foldline and pin the entire facing to the neck edge over the collar. The collar will be sandwiched between the facing and linen top. Pin the front edge of the left facing (#5) to the left front (#1). Stitch around the neck, and down the left front edge **(FIG. 11)**.

15 Before flipping the facings to the inside, stitch across the bottom 1" (2.5 cm) from the edge, stopping at the hem edge of the facings **(SEE FIG. 11)**.

16 Trim the seams and clip the curves. Finger fold the corner seam allowances at the stitching line **(FIG. 12)** and then turn the facings to the inside. "Pop" the corners out and smooth the curves. Press the seamed edges. TIP: *Folding the corner seams before turning makes a sharper corner than trimming the seam.*

17 Topstitch ⅛" (3 mm) around the neck seam under the collar to secure the facing **(FIG. 13)**.

18 Finishing: Press the hem under ¼" (6 mm) and again ¾" (2 cm) and secure with basting glue. Topstitch along the center of the soutache braid to catch the hem and left front facing.

19 Run an easing stitch in the cap of the sleeve and attach the sleeve to the armholes with right sides together. Trim the seam to ¼" (6 mm) and cover with bias, or roll and whip the raw edge **(FIG. 14)**.

20 Mark and stitch the buttonholes on the left front and buttons on the right front. Stitch a snap under each corner of the left front extension to keep the corners from curling. Stitch a clear snap at the neck center front and to the end of the left front extension under the collar **(FIG. 15)**.

21 Soak to remove the basting glue and markings. Air dry to slightly damp; press with steam and starch.

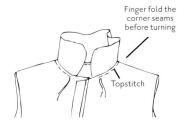

Fold corner seams

FIGURE 12

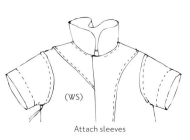

Finger fold the corner seams before turning

Topstitch

FIGURE 13

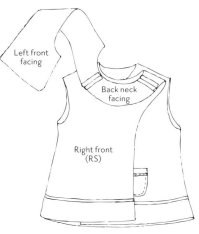

Left front facing

Back neck facing

Right front (RS)

FIGURE 10

(WS)

Attach sleeves

FIGURE 14

Facing (WS)

Right front (RS)

Left front (RS)

Facing (WS)

Stitch

1" (2.5 cm)

FIGURE 11

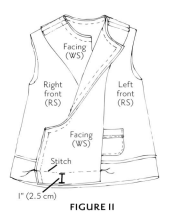

• Snaps   ○ Buttons

FIGURE 15

Belle Heir Shirt & Button-on Pants

CONSTRUCTION BY AMELIA JOHANSON

TREASURES ABOUND AT BELLE HEIR (*www.belleheir.com*) where vintage clothing for babies and children is paramount. Each piece is sweeter than the next, and we chose this little boy's top to reproduce just for our *Sew Beautiful* readers. The V-shaped yoke and piped tucks are design elements that are not only applicable to today's children's fashions, the overall style of the top could be worn by a boy or girl. We've made our reproduction with short sleeves and give you the option of the button-on shorts or the pull-ons from our Prince William pattern. The supply list includes what you will need for the original navy version as well as for the light blue and white suit we made using piqué and pre-tucked cotton.

What You'll Need...

PATTERNS

(available on the CD-rom)

"Belle Heir Tucked Shirt" (sizes 2 to 6)

"Button-on Shorts" (sizes 2 to 6)

"William's Pull-on Shorts" (sizes 2 to 4)

NOTE: *The pattern and instructions provided are for the short-sleeve option.*

NOTE: *The shorts pattern provided is a basic button-on design without front pockets. Sample shown in the photo are the pull-on shorts. You may use either the button-on pattern or pull-on pattern with this top.*

FABRIC

(size chart, layout guide, and yardage requirements available on the CD-rom)

Antique Version

  Navy and white striped cotton (for shirt and bindings)

  Navy cotton piqué (for piping and shorts)

OR White Cotton Version

  Swiss cotton sateen (for sleeves, collar, lining, front and back)

  Swiss pleated cotton (for collar, yoke, and cuffs) or you may opt to pleat your own fabric

  Light blue cotton piqué (for piping and shorts)

NOTIONS

Piping (can be purchased by the yard or made from shorts fabric)

Baby cord for piping if self-made (collar and tucks; optional for sleeve cuffs)

Four to five ⅜"–½" (1–1.3 cm) buttons

Six to eight ⅝"–1" (1.5–2.5 cm) buttons (for button-on shorts)

6"–8" (15–20.5 cm) of 1" (2.5 cm) wide elastic (for pull-on shorts)

⅛ yd (11.5 cm) of lightweight interfacing (for shirt collar, waistband of pull-on shorts, and yoke/facings)

SUPPLIES

Blue wash-away marking pen

Basting glue

Grid-lined quilting ruler

DARR piping ruler (optional for trimming seams)

What to Cut...

Navy Stripe Shirt

FROM COTTON STRIPE:

Two shirt fronts (Mark tuck lines and stopping points for tucks as indicated on pattern.)

Two front yoke/plackets

Two sleeves

Two collars (one is lining)

Two front yoke/plackets (for lining/facing) (Cut interfacing for each and fuse to wrong side.)

One shirt back on fold

One bias strip 1¼" × 7" (3.2 × 18 cm) (for back neck seam)

Two bias strips 2¼" (5.5 cm) × length of armscyes

Two sleeve cuff pieces 1¾" (4.5 cm) × the width of the sleeve cuff (optional)

FROM NAVY PIQUÉ

(for button-on shorts):

Four shorts fronts (two for lining)

Four shorts backs (two for lining)

1½" × 1¾ yd (3.8 × 160 cm) bias strip for self-piping

White Tucked Shirt

FROM SWISS COTTON SATEEN:

NOTE: *You may opt to pleat your own fabric for this option. Requires extra yardage for pleating. Create pleated yardage, then cut out pattern pieces.*

Two shirt fronts (Mark tuck lines and stopping points on pattern.)

Two sleeves

One collar (for lining)

Two front yoke/plackets for lining facing (Cut interfacing for each and fuse to wrong side.)

One shirt back on fold

One bias strip 1¼" × 7" (3.2 × 18 cm) for back neck seam)

FROM SWISS PLEATED COTTON

One collar

Two front yoke/plackets

Two sleeve cuff pieces (1¾" [4.5 cm] × width of sleeve [cuff is optional]).

FROM LIGHT BLUE LINEN

Two shorts fronts (four if lining)

Two shorts backs (four if lining)

Front waistband

1½" × 1¾ yd (3.8 × 160 cm) bias strip for self piping

FROM LIGHTWEIGHT INTERFACING

Front waistband

NOTE: *Layout guide on CD-rom does not reflect pleated fabric or color blocking options. If you plan to use varying fabrics, create a mock layout on paper to determine appropriate yardage for different fabrics.*

How to Make It...

Piped Tucks

1 Create enough piping to accommodate all six tucks, collar (and cuffs optional). Refer to Piping instructions in the Techniques section on page 124. Trim piping seam allowance to ¼" (6 mm) (a DARR piping ruler is perfect for this task). Cut six 4¼" (11 cm) long strips of piping.

2 Fold along the first tuck line (indicated by a dashed line on the pattern); press. Place the fold to the straight line and press the tuck all the way down.

3 Open the tuck and run a line of basting glue from the top edge to the marked dot. Position a piece of piping on the glue so that the stitching line of the piping is aligned to the straight line marked on the shirt. Begin at the marked dot and work upward; leave the excess piping extended at the top edge, which will be trimmed after stitching. For a clean end, cut the end of the piping piece at an angle

and bend the raw end to the inside of the tuck so that the curved end touches the marked dot **(FIG. 1)**. Finger press to secure the glue to the piping.

4 Flip the shirt over the piping so that the right sides are together and the piping is sandwiched between the fold. Stitch the tuck line, catching the piping seam allowance inside; stop at the marked dot, securing the end of the tuck and the end of the piping at the same time. Skip a distance and start stitching on second mark and continue to the bottom of the front shirt **(FIG. 2)**. Repeat for all six tucks. When complete, trim off the piping strips even with top edge.

Shirt Front

1 Stay-stitch (1.5 stitch length) on the ½" (1.3 cm) seamline in the corner of the pleated fabric yoke/placket piece where indicated by a square on the pattern. Clip the seam to the square **(FIG. 3)**.

2 Pin the front yoke/placket piece to the shirt front, right sides together. Start at the bottom of the shirt and stitch up to the corner and pivot. Stitch across the top **(FIG. 4)**. Flip away from the front and press the seam toward the yoke/placket. Repeat for the opposite side. Set the fronts aside.

Sleeves (Optional)

1 Turn up and hem the bottom of the sleeve, or apply a cuff as shown. For a cuffed sleeve, trim 1" (2.5 cm) from the bottom of the sleeve.

2 Stitch a strip of piping to the top edge of the cuff (if cut from the tucked fabric, the tucks will face down away from the top edge). Trim the seam to ¼" (6 mm) and press under.

3 Place the right side of the cuff to the wrong side of the sleeve and stitch a ¼" (6 mm) seam. Flip the cuff to the right side of the sleeve and press the seam. Glue-baste along the top edge and stitch in the ditch of the piping to secure the

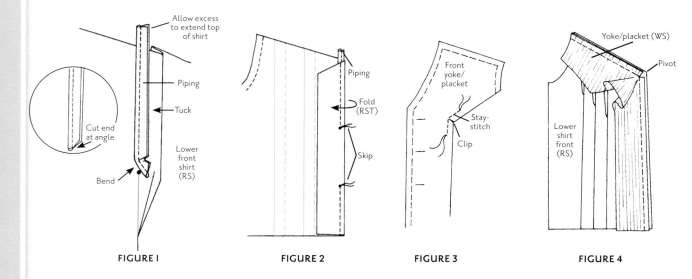

FIGURE 1

FIGURE 2

FIGURE 3

FIGURE 4

cuff **(FIG. 5)**. TIP: *Remove the cording from the piping ½" (1.3 cm) on each end to reduce the bulk in the seam.*

4 Run a row of ease stitches in the cap of the sleeve. Repeat to complete the other sleeve and set it aside for final construction.

Collar

1 Glue-baste and stitch the piping around the outer edge of the pleated fabric collar.

2 Stitch the cotton sateen collar lining to the collar with the right sides together, catching the piping in the ½" (1.3 cm) seam **(FIG. 6)**.

3 Trim the seam to ¼" (6 mm); notch the curves and turn and press the collar.

Construction

1 Stitch the fronts and back together at the shoulder seams. Press the shoulder seam allowance toward the front.

2 Pin the collar to the neck opening with the lining side of the collar to the right side of the shirt (pleated side facing up) **(FIG. 7)**.

3 Overcast or serge along the inside raw edge of the yoke/placket facing (lining piece). Press the shoulder seam to the wrong side ½" (1.3 cm). Pin the facing to the shirt front, right sides together, along the neck and front edges with the collar sandwiched between the facing and shirt layers (the shoulder seam on the facing remains pressed back). Now, pin the bias fabric strip over the collar, matching the raw edge at the back neck seam. Trim the ends of the bias ½" (1.3 cm) beyond the shoulder seams and place the bias ends over the facing piece. Stitch from the center back neckline to the front bottom edge on the left side. Repeat for the right side, working from the center to the bottom edge **(FIG. 8)**.

4 Trim and grade the seam. Flip the facing and bias to the inside of the shirt and press the neck and front placket seams. Fold under the remaining raw edge of the back neck bias and hand whip along the fold edge to enclose the seam. Hand whip the folded shoulder seam of the facing over the shoulder seam of the shirt (this also encloses the bias strip ends) **(FIG. 9)**.

5 Ease the cap of the sleeve by pulling on the bobbin thread of the ease stitch (do not gather, easing is to aid in fitting the sleeve into the armhole smoothly). Pin to the armscye right sides together and smooth out any gathers or possible tucks. Stitch the seam, trim and finish with a serger or zigzag.

6 Stitch the side seams of the shirt and sleeves **(FIG. 10)**. Finish the seam with a serger or zigzag. Press.

7 Serge or overcast stitch around the bottom of the garment.

8 Flip the front facings back to the garment right side at the bottom edge and pin in place. Stitch ¼" (6 mm) (just above the serged finish) **(FIG. 11)**. Flip the facing back to the inside of the garment. Press up the remainder of the hem edge, turning up the serged finish. Topstitch the facing and stitch the hem **(FIG. 12)**.

8 Mark and work the buttons and buttonholes to finish the front.

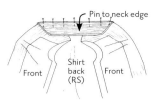

FIGURE 7

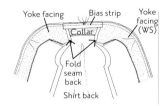

FIGURE 8

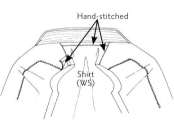

FIGURE 9

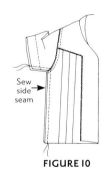

FIGURE 10

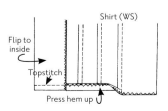

FIGURE 11

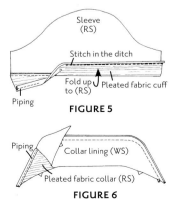

FIGURE 5

FIGURE 6

FIGURE 12

Button-on Shorts

1 Place the outer front pieces right sides together and stitch using a ¼" (6 mm) seam. Clip the curve. Repeat for the lining front pieces.

2 Place the back to each side of the front, right sides together. Using a ¼" (6 mm) seam, stitch, starting at the bottom of the pants and stopping at the dot. Repeat for the lining (**FIGS. 13 and 14**).

3 Place the lining to the outer pants, right sides together, pin along the top, plackets and hem.

4 Starting at the placket dot of the front, stitch from the dot up the placket, across the top of the pants, down the placket and to the dot (**FIG. 15**).

5 Along the back pants, stitch from the dot along the outer edge of the placket and across the top. Repeat for the other side (**FIG. 16**).

6 Trim away ⅛" (3 mm) of the lining at the hems (**FIG. 17**). This will make the lining turn up inside the pants leg after stitching.

7 Stitch the lining to the outer pants at the hems. This creates a tube. Clip and hem the curves (**FIG. 18**).

8 Place your hand between the lining and the outer pants; pull the back through to meet the back, lining- to-lining and outer-fabric-to-outer-fabric (**FIG. 19**). Pin in place.

9 Starting at the crotch, stitch the back seam in place leaving a 3" (7.5 cm) opening in the lining seam (**FIG. 20**). Clip the curves. This creates another tube at the crotch.

10 Reach through to the crotch and pull one through to the other (**FIG. 21**). Pin together, lining-to-lining and outer-fabric-to-outer-fabric. Stitch in place. You will be stitching in a circle (**FIG. 22**).

11 Close the opening by hand (**FIG. 23**). Press well.

12 Refer to the buttonhole placement on the pattern. Add buttonholes, fit the garment to the child, and sew buttons on the shirt where needed.

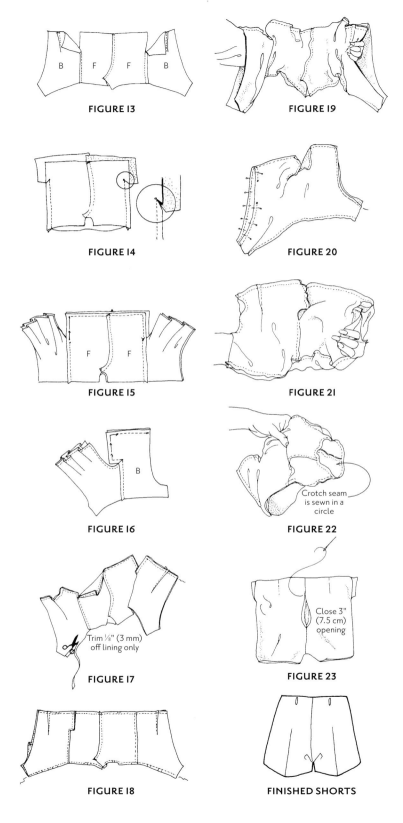

FIGURE 13

FIGURE 19

FIGURE 14

FIGURE 20

FIGURE 15

FIGURE 21

FIGURE 16

Crotch seam is sewn in a circle

FIGURE 22

FIGURE 17

Trim ⅛" (3 mm) off lining only

FIGURE 23

Close 3" (7.5 cm) opening

FIGURE 18

FINISHED SHORTS

Edward's Sailor Bubble

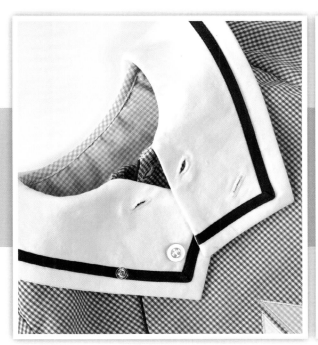

*I*N 1846, QUEEN VICTORIA ORDERED A SAILOR SUIT made for 4-year-old Prince Albert Edward to wear on the royal yacht. So endearing was the child in his scaled-down uniform that he was immortalized in a portrait by Franz Xaver Winterhalter. Thus began the allure of nautical-inspired clothing, a perennial favorite for more than 150 years.

We've created a modified sailor collar we call the "Ascot Collar" to work perfectly with one of our favorite bubble patterns. Because the bubble has an asymmetrical front opening, the collar does, too. The boy's bubble is embellished with a sailboat appliqué, but we've also included a ducky appliqué template on the CD-rom pattern sheet, and a gathered sleeve pattern on the CD-rom in case a little pink sailor bubble would better suit your little one.

What You'll Need...

PATTERNS
(available on the CD-rom)

"Edward's Sailor Bubble" (sizes 6, 12, and 24 mos.)

Sailboat (or Sailing Duck) Appliqué

FABRIC
(layout guide provided on the CD-rom)

1–1¼ yd (91.5–114.5 cm) of royal microcheck for main garment

1–1¼ yd (91.5–114.5 cm) of light blue microcheck for lining and appliqué

½ yd (45.5 cm) of white cotton broadcloth for collar, cuffs, and appliqué

TRIM

One package Wrights Yale blue double-fold bias for collar trim, appliqué, and piping

1¾ yd (160 cm) of baby piping cord

Package of ⅜" (1 cm) wide elastic

Seven buttons ⅜"–½" (1–1.3 cm)

SUPPLIES

Sulky Machine Embroidery Thread (in colors to match appliqué fabrics)

Wonder-Under

Lightweight interfacing

Crafter's Choice basting glue by API

4.0/80 twin needle (optional)

Edge/joining foot (optional)

Clear snaps

Blue wash-away marking pen

What to Cut...

FROM THE MAIN FABRIC
(royal microcheck)

One left garment front

One block for right garment front larger than pattern piece

One garment back

Two sleeves

FROM THE LINING FABRIC
(light blue microcheck)

Two garment fronts

One garment back

Small square for boat appliqué

FROM BROADCLOTH
(white)

Four collar fronts

Two collar backs

Small square for boat appliqué

FROM DOUBLE-FOLD BIAS

5" (12.5 cm) piece pressed open for boat appliqué

8" (20.5 cm) piece for inside tab

1¼ yd (114.5 cm) strip pressed open for piping

1⅛ yd (93.8 cm) for collar trim

NOTE: *If choosing the Sailing Duck Appliqué, use pressed-open double bias tape for the boat to match piping. Use small pieces of yellow broadcloth for the duck, orange broadcloth for the beak, and white broadcloth for the hat. Securely stitch on a sew-on eye to finish.*

BABY SIZE CHART

Size 6 mos.

    Chest 18" (43 cm)

    Wt. 13–16 lbs. (5.89–7.25 kg)

    Ht. 25"–26" (63.5–66 cm)

Size 12 mos.

    Chest 19" (48.5 cm)

    Wt. 19–21 lbs. (8.61–9.52 kg)

    Ht. 27"–28" (68.5–71 cm)

Size 24 mos.

    Chest 21" (53.5 cm)

    Wt. 26–29 lbs. (11.79–13.51kg)

    Ht. 31"–32" (79–81.5 cm)

How to Make It…

Sailboat Appliqué

NOTE: *Whether you choose to appliqué or embroider your bubble front by hand or machine, trace off the front pattern piece first on a larger block of fabric before embellishing, especially if you need to hoop the fabric.*

1 Back the small pieces of the three different appliqué fabrics with Wonder-Under. Using sailboat appliqué from CD-rom, trace off a white sail, a print sail, and a solid-colored boat. (On the garment shown, purchased bias tape was pressed open, backed with Wonder-Under and used as boat fabric to create an exact match with trim and piping.)

2 Peel off Wonder-Under backing and position boat pieces on center of bubble front (traced-off right side) centered about 6" (15 cm) down from the neck edge (**FIG. 1**) and adjacent to the side curve.

3 When satisfied with your placement, cover the appliqué with an iron set to cotton setting. Do not twist or move the iron, simply press down to avoid the moving placement of the appliqué.

4 Using Sulky machine embroidery thread to match each appliqué section and a narrow machine appliqué, stitch around each shape. Refer to the Techniques section on page 124 for basic appliqué instructions.

5 Check the traced margins with the right front pattern piece. Retrace if necessary and cut out.

Bubble Construction

Seam allowances are ⅝" (1.5 cm).

1 Press your bias tape open and create enough piping to stitch around the right front curved edge and across two sleeves cuffs (set the sleeve piping aside). Refer to Piping in the Techniques section on page 124 if needed. Stitch the piping to the embellished right front piece along the curved edge. Clip the seam allowance on the piping where needed to curve around the pattern piece.

2 Join the front bubble pieces to the back bubble at the side seams (**FIG. 2**).

3 Fold a 8" (20.5 cm) piece of bias tape in half lengthwise and edge-stitch. Loop in half and position it 1½" (3.8 cm) below the underarm seam on the right side of the right back lining piece (this strip secures the bottom flap with a snap). Baste the strip to secure (**FIG. 3**). Assemble the front and back linings at the side seams in the same manner as the bubble, catching the bias tape loop in the seam.

4 Place the lining to the bubble bodice with right sides together and stitch along the front edges and across the bottom (**FIG. 4**). Turn the bubble right side out and press the seams.

5 Topstitch 1/16" (2 mm) from the bottom edge along the legs and crotch seam (**FIG. 5**).

6 Stitch again ⅜" (1 cm) from the bottom edge along the leg opening to form a casing (**FIG. 6**).

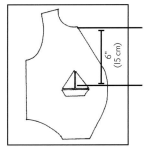

FIGURE 1

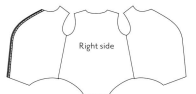

Right side

FIGURE 2

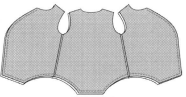

Back lining

FIGURE 3

FIGURE 4

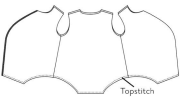

Topstitch

FIGURE 5

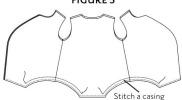

Stitch a casing

FIGURE 6

7 Cut a piece of elastic for each leg: 7½" (19 cm) for size 6 months and 8" (20.5 cm) for sizes 12 to 24 months.

8 Slip elastic between the bubble fabric and lining by going through the top opening. With a safety pin or bodkin, guide the elastic through the casing channel between the layers. Stop when the end of the elastic aligns with the front end of the casing; pin and tack stitch with a back-and-forth straight stitch to secure the end of the elastic inside (**FIG. 7**).

9 Continue running elastic through to the other end; pin to secure. Remove the safety pin or bodkin and tack-stitch the end as before (**FIG. 8**).

10 Sew the shoulder seams of the bubble and bubble lining separately with right sides together. Press the shoulder seams open and place the layers together, aligning the shoulder seams.

Ascot Collar

1 Using the collar pattern, mark the dots on the collar fronts with a wash-away marking pen.

2 Apply interfacing to the collar pieces. Stitch the collar fronts to the collar back. Press the seams open (**FIG. 9**). With a wash-away marking pen, draw a line ½" (1.3 cm) from the seam allowance starting at the inside edge of one front continuing around the back collar and ending at the inside edge of the opposite front (**FIG. 10**).

3 Glue-baste single-fold bias tape or spaghetti bias along the placement line created in Step 2, mitering at the corners (**FIG. 11**). NOTE: *On the garment shown, bias tape was used for piping, trim, and boat appliqué to create an exact match; you could also use spaghetti bias with matching yardage for the piping and appliqué.*

4 Stitch along each side of the applied bias trim using thread to match, an edge/joining foot and left needle position, or use a twin needle.

5 Join the front collar linings to the back collar lining. Press the seams open. Place the trimmed collar to the lining collar wrong sides together and stitch around all the edges except the neck edge starting and stopping at the dots marked in Step 1. Clip across the seam allowance to the dots. Turn the collar right side out. Carefully push out corners and press.

6 The seam allowance above the clip/dots should extend out. Stay-stitch around the neckline of the collar to hold both layers together (**FIG. 12**).

7 Pin the collar to the garment neck edge aligning the seams at the shoulders. Stitch to apply.

8 Finish the neck edge with a bias binding. Refer to the Techniques section on page 124 if necessary.

9 Place the right side of the collar over the left side of the collar aligning the trim into a V. Pin. Mark one buttonhole ½" (1.3 cm) from the center neckline edge on both collars and top garment layer. Mark a second buttonhole ½" (1.3 cm) above the trim point on the bottom of the top collar (**FIG. 13**).

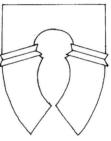

FIGURE 9

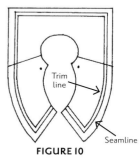

Trim line

Seamline

FIGURE 10

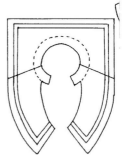

Bias trim

FIGURE 11

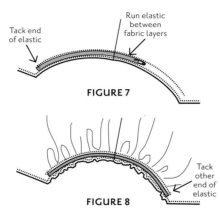

Tack end of elastic

Run elastic between fabric layers

FIGURE 7

Tack other end of elastic

FIGURE 8

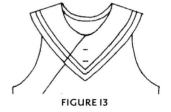

FIGURE 12

FIGURE 13

Sleeves

1. Cut off the sleeve hem on the foldline. Place piping to one raw edge of the 2" (5 cm) cuff strip with right sides together and raw edges even. Stitch just inside the piping stitch line (**FIG. 14**). Press the seam allowance down. Using the sleeve pattern, trace the sleeve seam angles on each end of the cuff and cut out (**FIG. 15**).

2. Place the right side of the cuff to the wrong side of the sleeve, so that the unpiped raw edge is even with the sleeve raw edge; stitch with a ⅝" (1.5 cm) seam (**FIG. 16**). Trim the seam to ¼" (6 mm). Press the cuff to the right side of the sleeve so that ¼" (6 mm) of the cuff is still to the inside. Turn under the piping seam allowance and topstitch the cuff to the sleeve just below the piping trim. Stitch the sleeve seam (**FIG. 17**).

3. Run an ease stitch in the sleeve cap to ease it into the armhole. (For a girl's puffed sleeve, run two rows of gathering stitches to gather it.) Stitch the sleeves into the armholes treating the bubble and lining as one layer. Trim the seam and finish with a zigzag, overcast, or serge the edge.

4. Place both front flaps together at the crotch and topstitch across the bottom to secure the layers together (**FIG. 18**).

5. Mark and stitch out three buttonholes through the top layers and corresponding buttons on the back.

6. Place two or three buttons and buttonholes along the front curve of the bubble (refer to main photo for placement). NOTE: *The front flap can be closed in many creative ways.*

7. Sew a clear snap to the bias loop on the inside and to the right side of the bottom front flap curve to secure the flap inside.

8. Stitch out the buttonholes marked on the collar, taking extra care that they align on each layer (**FIG. 19**). Stitch one button on the bottom layer of the bubble front and a second button on the left collar (**FIG. 20**). To ensure the trim stays aligned, stitch a plastic snap where the trim meets under the collar edge.

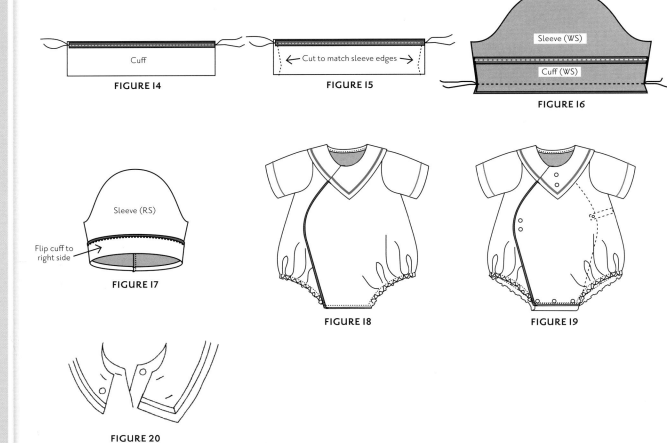

FIGURE 14

FIGURE 15

FIGURE 16

FIGURE 17

Flip cuff to right side

FIGURE 18

FIGURE 19

FIGURE 20

SEWING
Christening Accessories

CHRISTENING ACCESSORIES, LIKE THE ELABORATE GOWNS they accompany, carry with them just as much sentiment, sometimes more, as the bonnets, bibs, booties, and blankets can be used through generations more easily than a gown that is constructed to fit. We've selected a collection of accessory patterns so that you can complete your baby's christening ensembles in heirloom fashion. From the adorable lace boots based on a gift sent to a royal baby to the Boutis bonnet created with an age-old French technique, each piece is a treasure. To help you keep special items safe, we've also included instructions for making a Christening Accessories Holder.

Royal Christening Bonnet

BY CHERYL R. DAVIDSON

THE ROYAL CHRISTENING GOWN MAY BE A PRICELESS treasure, worn by generations of princes and princesses, but the inspiration bonnet we chose to pair with it cost a mere fifty cents at an estate sale. With its distinctive Victorian style in a combination of ribbon and netting, the remake is the perfect mate for our variation of the royal gown. The bonnet pattern is provided on the CD-rom in sizes NB to 9 months, and the embroidery diagrams can be found in the Techniques section on page 124.

What You'll Need...

PATTERNS
(available on the CD-rom)

"Royal Christening Bonnet" (sizes NB to 9 mo.)

Embroidery Stitch Diagrams in Techniques section on page 124.

FABRIC
½ yd (45.5 cm) of ivory cotton netting

⅜ yd (34.5 cm) of ecru silk batiste (lining) or use a color to match ribbon of choice

LACE AND TRIM
1¼ yd (114.5 cm) of ⅝" wide (1.5 cm) ecru lace edging

2 yd (183 cm) of ⅝" wide (1.5 cm) ballet pink silk/satin ribbon

⅜ yd (34.5 cm) of ecru entredeux

THREAD
DMC Six-Strand Cotton Embroidery Floss

> #818 baby pink
>
> #819 lt baby pink
>
> #899 md rose
>
> #503 md blue green

SUPPLIES
Fabric-marking pen

Quilting thread, ivory

40 wt Isacord embroidery thread (#2160-pink)

Sulky Solvy water-soluble stabilizer

5" (12.5 cm) hand-embroidery hoop

NOTE: *Wash netting and silk lining to soften and shrink. Press dry once damp.*

What to Cut...

FROM NETTING
Rectangular piece for top of bonnet 16½" × 8¼" (42 × 21 cm) for sizes 0 to 3 mo., and 18½" × 9" (47 × 23 cm) for size 6 to 9 mo.

5" × 36" (12.5 × 91.5 cm) piece for ruffle

FROM SILK
Bonnet front

Crown circle

Block large enough to hoop for embroidered second crown circle

How to Make It...

Seam allowances are ⅜" (34.5 cm).

TIP: *Use a strip of water-soluble stabilizer under netting for easier handling while stitching.*

1 Use quilting thread and baste a line of stitching ⅜" (34.5 cm) from the front long edge of the netting rectangle. Starting 1¾" (4.5 cm) from basting, mark a line for the first tuck. Measure 1¼" (3.2 cm) from the first tuck line three more times for a total of four tuck lines.

2 Fold the netting on the tuck lines and stitch ⅛" (3 mm) tucks with quilting thread and a 3.0 stitch length; leave tails at the ends of each row to draw up later.

3 With quilting thread and a 3.0 stitch length, stitch a ¼" (6 mm) hem along the back raw edge, leaving a thread tail to draw up later. Remove or soak to dissolve water-soluble stabilizer if used before you gather tucks and edges.

4 Pull threads in each row and distribute the gathers evenly to fit the bonnet front pattern piece. Carefully pull out the tail threads to tie off along the neck and back seam of the bonnet pattern (do not tie off the thread on the back edge of the bonnet, this will be pulled later). Cut off the excess netting following the neck and back edges of the pattern (**FIG. 1**). Stay-stitch along the seamlines.

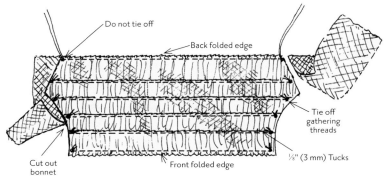

FIGURE 1

5 Join the back seam with a French seam.

6 Pull up the back threads to gather the back hole, leaving about a 1" (2.5 cm) window for the crown embroidery to peek through from the lining; see back-view photograph.

7 Cut two strips of entredeux—one for the front edge and one for the neck edge. Stitch the entredeux to the front seam and the neck seam of the netting bonnet with right sides together, using a ⅜" (1 cm) seam allowance and stitching in the ditch of the entredeux. Do not roll and whip the seam. Set the netting bonnet aside.

8 Hoop a square of silk fabric and hand embroider the roses for the crown following the Embroidery instructions provided on page 86.

9 Trace the bonnet crown circle pattern around the embroidery with the embroidery centered; cut out.

10 Run gathering stitches ¼" (6 mm) from the back edge of the silk bonnet lining.

11 Sew the back seam of the silk bonnet lining with a French seam.

12 With right sides together, gather and pin the back of the silk lining to the plain silk crown circle and stitch. Press the seam toward the crown center **(FIG. 2)**.

13 Stitch a row of stay-stitching ⅜" (1 cm) from the edge of the embroidered crown circle. Pull up the stitching slightly to cup the seam; press the seam to the inside of the crown and form a neatly pressed circle. Place the embroidered crown over the bonnet lining crown and hand whip around the seam **(FIG. 3)**.

14 Pin the netting bonnet and the silk lining right sides together with the entredeux sandwiched between the layers. Stitch the seam, leaving 3" (7.5 cm) open on the neck edge for turning **(FIG. 4)**. Trim the seam and roll and whip with a zigzag. Turn the bonnet right side out. Press the seam away from the entredeux.

15 Hand-stitch the opening closed.

16 Trim off the remaining fabric tape from the entredeux. Gather the lace edging and butt and zigzag to the edge of the entredeux **(FIG. 5)**.

17 For the netting ruffle, spray starch on the netting strip and place on the water-soluble stabilizer while still damp. Press with a dry iron to fuse to the stabilizer. Trace a 2" (5 cm) strip along the center of the netting but do not cut out.

18 Thread the machine with pink Isacord embroidery thread and select a narrow scallop stitch. Stitch the scallop along each edge and each end of netting following the traced lines. Carefully cut along the scallop edge **(FIG. 6)**. Rinse thoroughly to remove the marks and stabilizer. Press the strip.

19 Stitch a long basting stitch lengthwise along the center of the strip. Gather the strip to fit the front of the bonnet and pin over the lace ruffle. Place the stitching line of the strip along the entredeux of the bonnet front and zigzag stitch in place.

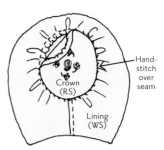

Hand-stitch over seam

Crown (RS)

Lining (WS)

FIGURE 3

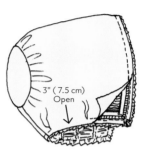

3" (7.5 cm) Open

FIGURE 4

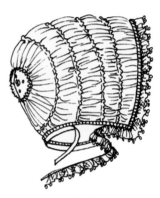

FIGURE 5

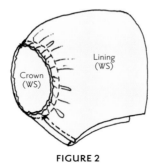

Crown (WS)

Lining (WS)

FIGURE 2

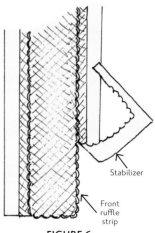

Stabilizer

Front ruffle strip

FIGURE 6

Ribbon Trim

1. Cut a piece of ribbon to fit across the front ruffle plus ½" (1.3 cm) for turning ends under. Place the ribbon over a piece of water-soluble stabilizer and secure it in a hand-embroidery hoop. Embroider the roses following the Embroidery instructions provided on page 124.

2. Remove the stabilizer from the ribbon and pin over the netting ruffle centering the middle rose. Tack with tiny French knots using one strand of baby pink floss.

3. Turn the raw ribbon ends under and secure with a machine straight stitch.

4. To make chin ties, cut the remaining ribbon in half. Hand-stitch a triple-loop bow on one end of each strip. Tack to the front corners of the bonnet.

Embroidery
Ribbon Band

Embroider rosebuds on the bow using photo for guide.

Embroider three full bullion roses on the crown starting at the center front.

Stitch the remaining two roses 2½" (5.6 cm) from each side of the center.

Stitch three stemmed rosebuds ½" (1.3 cm) apart between the roses.

Stitch three medium pink floss rosebuds with green bullion leaves on the triple-loop bows tacked to each corner.

Crown

Center a full bullion rose starting with three medium rose floss bullions. Stitch five baby pink floss bullion knots around the center. Finish with seven light baby pink floss bullions. Stitch one green floss bullion at the bottom of the rose for the leaf.

Stitch four stemmed rosebuds in a circle around the center rose. The stem is a backstitch, and the leaves are made with two tiny bullions in green floss. The rosebuds are made with two tiny bullions in medium rose floss.

NOTE: *Refer to the Techniques section on page 124 for stitch diagrams.*

Victoria & Albert Lace Boots

by Sivje Parish

V & A images/Victoria & Albert Museum

THESE ADORABLE LACE BOOTS were part of an elaborate collection gifted to Her Royal Highness Princes Mary of York, great granddaughter of Queen Victoria, while expecting her first child. The baby, however was a boy, born on February 7, 1923, so the gift was returned with a gracious thank-you note and the set now resides in the Victoria & Albert Museum of Childhood in pristine condition.

Based on the photograph, Sivje Parish drafted a pattern and instructions so your little princess can have her own pair of royal lace boots.

What You'll Need...

PATTERN
(available on the CD-rom)

"Lace Boot" (sizes 0 to 2)

Sole

Boot upper

Tongue

FABRIC

⅜ yd (34.5 cm) of China silk

¼ yd (23 cm) of lace fabric

¼ yd (23 cm) of Swiss flannel

TRIM

2 yd (183 cm) of silk ribbon

¾ yd (69 cm) of ½" wide (1.3 cm) gathered lace edging

SUPPLIES

Thread

¼ yd (23 cm) of fusible interfacing (Dream Weave)

Wash-away marking pen

What to Cut...

FROM SILK

Four bootie uppers on the fold

Four tongues

Two 6" (15 cm) squares for the bootie soles

FROM LACE FABRIC

Two bootie uppers on the fold

FROM FLANNEL

Two bootie uppers on the fold

Two tongues

One 6" (15 cm) square for the bootie soles

FROM INTERFACING

One 6" (15 cm) square for bootie soles

FROM RIBBON

Eight 9" (23 cm) long ties

How to Make It...

Seam allowances are a scant ¼" (6 mm).

Transfer any pattern markings to pieces with wash-away marking pen.

1. After cutting bootie lining uppers on fold, open and lay out flat. To create the quilted lining, take two silk bootie lining uppers and two flannel lining uppers. Lay one silk upper on top of one flannel upper, matching the edges exactly. Pin the two layers together. Starting at the center, where it was folded, machine stitch from the top edge to the bottom edge. Repeat this every ½" (1.3 cm) on either side of the first row of stitches until you have the entire piece stitched with straight rows ½" (1.3 cm) apart **(FIG. 1)**.

2. Starting at the top left corner, stitch diagonally to the bottom edge of the boot upper. Repeat at ½" (1.3 cm) intervals until the whole upper is stitched with diagonal rows. Repeat this with the second bootie upper and flannel **(FIG. 2)**.

3. Fold your quilted bootie upper lining pieces so that the silk is to the inside. Stitch the front top of the toe area. Press this seam flat. Repeat with the second quilted upper lining piece **(FIG. 3)**. Turn your upper so the silk side is out. Set aside.

4. Place one lace bootie upper to one silk bootie upper piece, matching the edges. Pin together and stitch all the edges together **(FIG. 4)**.

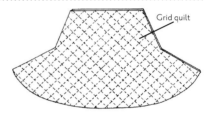

Grid quilt

FIGURE 2

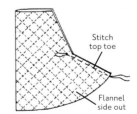

Stitch top toe

Flannel side out

FIGURE 3

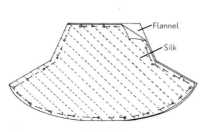

Flannel

Silk

FIGURE 1

Silk

Lace

FIGURE 4

5 Pin the lace edging to the front opening edge of the bootie upper, along the top, and down the other side of the front opening edge. Align the header edge of the lace to the seamline of the bootie (scalloped edge of lace faces away from the seam). Zigzag stitch in place along the header of the lace (**FIG. 5**).

6 Pin one ribbon tie at each "X" on the front edge openings of each bootie upper and stitch in place.

7 Just like you did in Step 3 (refer to **FIG. 3**) fold the lace bootie upper so that the lace is to the inside. Stitch the front top of the toe area. Open the seam and press lightly.

8 Layer two silk tongue pieces right sides together and then top with one flannel piece. Stitch around the outer edge leaving the bottom open. Press. Carefully clip the seam allowance at the rounded edges (**FIG. 6**). Turn so that the silk pieces are on the outside and the flannel is sandwiched inside. Press again.

9 Stitch diagonal rows from the rounded top of the tongue down to the bottom. Repeat from the other direction, creating a diamond quilting pattern. Stitch the bottom edge closed (**FIG. 7**). Repeat with second tongue pieces.

10 Pick up one quilted tongue and one quilted lining upper. Position the flat bottom of the tongue across the seam, about 1¼" (3.2 mm) to 1½" (3.8 cm) from the rounded edge of the front of the toe. Stitch across the bottom of the tongue to hold it in place (**FIG. 8**).

11 With the quilted lining upper piece right side out, fit the lace/silk upper piece over it, so that the lace is inside. Pin the front opening and the top edge of the lining to the front of the lace/silk upper. Pin the top edge of the lining to the top edge of the lace and silk upper. Make sure that the ribbon ties are stuffed inside

and the lace is pinned out of the way. Pull the tongue to the bottom opening of the boot (**FIG. 9**).

12 NOTE: *This is a very snug area to stitch, so please be careful.* Starting at the right front opening edge, stitch ¼" (6 mm) seam to the corner, rounding slightly, across the top edge to the left corner, rounding slightly again, and down the left front opening edge. Stitch as close to the front seam as you can without catching the scallop of the lace edging or ribbon ties. Carefully clip the seam allowance. Press the seam and turn so that the lace is on the outside and the lace edging is extending from the seam.

13 Pull the tongue back inside the boot so that it is behind the front opening edges. Hand-stitch the base of the front opening edge to the tongue (**FIG. 10**).

14 For your bootie soles, fuse the 6" (15 cm) square of interfacing to one layer of silk. Place the silk side down and then layer the 6" (15 cm) square of flannel; top that with the final 6" (15 cm) square of silk. Pin them together. Quilt with a diagonal grid of straight stitching, about ⅜" (1 cm) apart (**FIG. 11**).

15 Cut out two sole pieces from the quilted square.

16 Take one bootie upper and turn it lining side out again. Carefully fit one sole to the bottom edge of the bootie upper, pinning all around (**FIG. 12**). Carefully, stitch the sole to the bootie upper all the way around with a ¼" (6 mm) seam allowance. Finish the seam with a zigzag stitch. Turn the bootie lace side out.

17 Tie the ribbons in bows and cut off the excess ribbon.

Your lace boots are now ready for little feet.

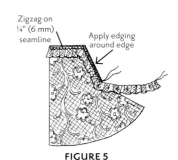

Zigzag on ¼" (6 mm) seamline

Apply edging around edge

FIGURE 5

Tongue

Silk

Flannel

FIGURE 6

Turn and quilt

FIGURE 7

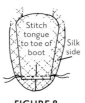

Stitch tongue to toe of boot

Silk side

Flannel side of lining

Silk of lace side

Pull tongue out

Stitch boot edge

Ribbons are tucked inside

FIGURE 8 **FIGURE 9**

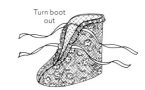

Turn boot out

FIGURE 10

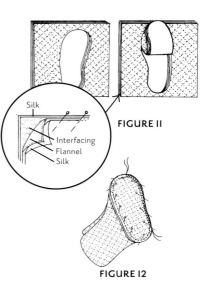

Silk

Interfacing

Flannel

Silk

FIGURE 11

FIGURE 12

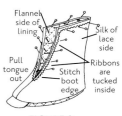

Duchess Baby Booties

PRECIOUS BOOTIES WITH A LACE FLOURISH on the toe dress up tiny feet for special occasions. The pair is made of comfy Swiss flannel and edged with a fabric bias binding. Silk satin ribbons are folded in half and secured with a button to create a double-layer ribbon tie.

What You'll Need...

PATTERN
(available on the CD-rom)

"Duchess Baby Booties" (sizes 0 to 2)

  Tied bootie upper

  Bootie sole

FABRIC

¼ yd (23 cm) of 60" wide (152.5 cm) white Swiss flannel

TRIM

2 yd of ¼" (6 mm) wide white silk satin ribbon

½ yd (183 cm) of ½" wide (1.3 cm) white lace edging

SUPPLIES

Six shank-style pearl buttons, ⅜" (1 cm)

60 wt cotton sewing thread

Size 70 universal machine needle for construction

Glass-head pins

Small hand-sewing needle

Water-soluble marking pen

Mini iron (optional)

What to Cut...

FROM SWISS FLANNEL

Four tied bootie uppers on the fold (two linings)

Four bootie soles (two soles and two linings)

Two bias strips, 1" × 9" (2.5 × 23 cm)

BOOTIE MEASUREMENT CHART

Size	Foot Length
0	Up to 3" (7.5 cm)
1	Up to 3½" (9 cm)
2	Up to 4" (10 cm)

How to Make It...

Seam allowances are ¼" (6 mm) unless otherwise noted.

Bootie Construction

1 At the center back, with right sides together, stitch the back seams of each bootie upper (**FIG. 1**).

2 Press the back seams open.

3 Place two bootie upper pieces, wrong sides together, and baste along the top edge (slightly less than a ¼" [6 mm] seam allowance) (**FIG. 2**). Repeat for the remaining two bootie uppers.

4 Reinforce the "V" at the center front of each upper by straight-stitching (L=1.5–2.0) 1" (2.5 cm) on each side of the "V" at the seamline.

5 Fold each 1" wide (2.5 cm) bias binding in half and press.

6 Beginning and ending slightly beyond the center front "V", place one folded bias band to the upper edge of the bootie upper, right sides together and matching the raw edges. Stitch the band to the bootie with a ¼" (6 mm) seam (**FIG. 3**). Trim the seam to ⅛" (3 mm).

7 Press the band up toward the raw edge of the bootie. Turn under the bias ends to miter, trimming as necessary.

8 Fold the bias band to the inside of the bootie, matching the fold to the stitching line. Hand whip in place. The seam allowance should fully "stuff" the band, creating a smooth bias band. Place a fabric marker "dot" on the lining side of the bootie. Mark the ribbon placement "X's" on each side of the bootie (**FIG. 4**).

9 Repeat Steps 6–8 for the remaining bootie and bias band.

10 Turn the bootie lining side out. Treating the two upper layers as one, pin one sole to the bottom edge of the bootie, right side of the sole to

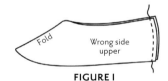

FIGURE 1

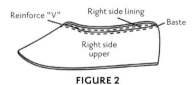

FIGURE 2

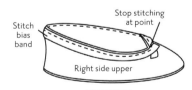

FIGURE 3

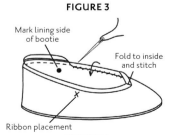

FIGURE 4

the right side of the upper. Stitch all the way around the sole **(FIG. 5)**.

11 With right sides together, pin the remaining sole over the upper lining, sandwiching both upper layers between the soles. Stitch, leaving a 1½" (3.8 cm) opening along one side (near the toe) for turning **(FIG. 6)**.

12 Clip the curves around the bootie very close to the stitching at ⅛" (3 mm) intervals **(FIG. 7)**. Trim the seam allowance to ⅛" (3 mm) all the way around except at the opening.

13 Turn the bootie through the opening. Turn the unstitched area to the inside. Stitch the opening closed **(FIG. 8)**. This will be the lining side of the bootie. Turn the bootie right side out (with lining inside). Press the sole seam.

14 Repeat Steps 10–13 for the second bootie.

Lace Rosettes and Ribbon Ties

1 Cut the lace edging into two 9" (23 cm) lengths.

2 Create a lace rosette from each lace piece by placing the cut ends right sides together to form a circle; stitch using a tiny, tight zigzag **(FIG. 9)**. Pull the gathering thread in the heading of the lace at the cut ends. Tie the pulled threads together.

3 On the wrong side of the rosette, hand-stitch back and forth across the open circle to further secure the center of the rosette **(FIG. 10)**.

4 Hand-stitch the lace rosettes to the toe of the booties **(FIG. 11A)**. Hand-stitch a button at the center of each rosette **(FIG. 11B)**.

5 Cut the silk satin ribbon into four equal lengths.

6 Fold one piece of ribbon in half. Hand-tack the fold of the ribbon in place at the "X" **(FIG. 12)**.

7 Repeat Step 2 for the remaining three ribbons.

8 Stitch a button on top of each ribbon near the fold **(FIG. 13)**.

9 Tie doubled ribbons into bows and cut the ends at an angle to the desired length. Tie a knot near the end of each ribbon **(FIG. 14)**.

NOTE: *When sewing buttons on baby garments, use double thread and knot securely to ensure they don't come loose.*

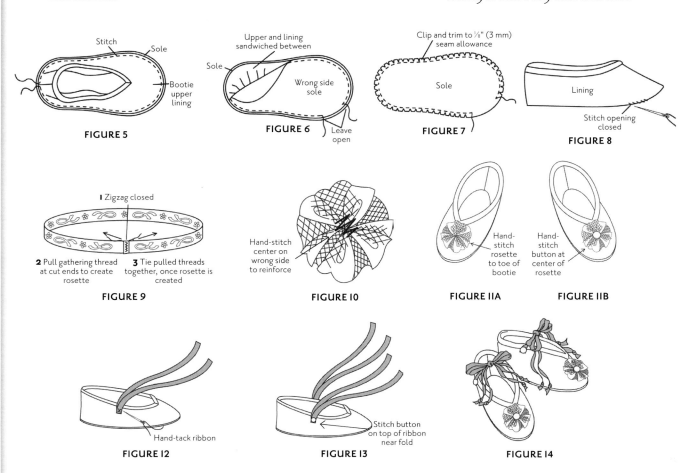

FIGURE 5
Stitch
Sole
Bootie upper lining

FIGURE 6
Upper and lining sandwiched between
Sole
Wrong side sole
Leave open

FIGURE 7
Clip and trim to ⅛" (3 mm) seam allowance
Sole

FIGURE 8
Lining
Stitch opening closed

FIGURE 9
1 Zigzag closed
2 Pull gathering thread at cut ends to create rosette
3 Tie pulled threads together, once rosette is created

FIGURE 10
Hand-stitch center on wrong side to reinforce

FIGURE 11A
Hand-stitch rosette to toe of bootie

FIGURE 11B
Hand-stitch button at center of rosette

FIGURE 12
Hand-tack ribbon

FIGURE 13
Stitch button on top of ribbon near fold

FIGURE 14

Baby John Cap & Booties

BY CHERYL R. DAVIDSON

ADD A BILL TO A CLASSIC BONNET DESIGN and you have a dapper little cap for a baby boy. Here the color scheme is blue and white, but you could easily substitute white or ecru trim, ribbon and lining for a more traditional christening ensemble. This particular design can be made plain and simple as shown; the open areas could be adorned with embroidery; or, to match our Little Boy Blue gown, shark's teeth sections could be joined with the entredeux beading. The precious booties were designed to match, and both patterns are provided on the CD-rom.

What You'll Need...

PATTERN
(available on the CD-rom)

"Baby John Cap and Booties" (cap size 6 mos, booties size 2)

FABRIC

¼ yd (23 cm) of white Swiss baby flannel

¼ yd (23 cm) of blue satin batiste for lining

TRIM AND LACE

1¼ yd (114.5 cm) of blue picot trim (cap and booties)

⅜ yd of entredeux beading

1½ yd of ⅝" (1.5 cm) blue silk-satin ribbon

⅜ yd (40.5 cm) of ⅛" (3 mm) blue silk-satin ribbon for beading

1 yd (91.5 cm) of ¼" (6 mm) blue silk satin ribbon for booties

8" (20.5 cm) piece of blue baby piping

SUPPLIES

Size 60 or 70 machine sewing needle

Mettler 60 wt thread (white)

Blue sewing thread

Clear filament thread

Wash-away mechanical pencil

What to Cut...

FROM SWISS FLANNEL

Two cap bills

Cap crown

Cap front

Two booties

Four bootie soles (two left; two right)

FROM SATIN BATISTE

Cap front

Cap crown

Two bootie soles (one right; one left)

Two bootie soles (repeated)

How to Make It...

Baby John Cap Construction

Seam allowances are ¼" (6 mm).

1 Separate the cap along the line indicated on the pattern for entredeux beading **(FIG. 1)**.

2 Using 60 wt thread and a ¼" (6 mm) seam allowance on each side, insert entredeux beading by stitching in the ditch of the entredeux. Trim the seam allowance and roll and whip the seams. Weave ⅛" (3 mm) blue ribbon through the beading **(FIG. 2)**.

3 Sew the center back seam of the bonnet.

4 Sew an ease stitch (L=3.0) along the seamline of the cap hole.

5 Sew an ease stitch around the seamline of the circle crown piece.

6 Ease the crown into the cap and hand-baste, then machine stitch the crown into the cap hole.

7 Repeat Steps 3–6 with the lining pieces.

8 Thread the machine with clear thread and carefully stitch blue picot trim around the crown seam on the right side of the flannel cap. The picots should point away from the center circle. Stitch with a very narrow zigzag along the edge of the trim **(FIG. 3)**.

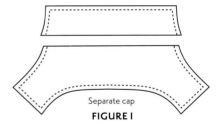

Separate cap
FIGURE 1

Add insertion and ribbon
FIGURE 2

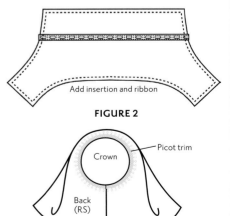

Crown

Picot trim

Back (R.S)

FIGURE 3

9 Cut a piece of blue piping to fit the front cap bill. Refer to Piping in the Techniques section on page 124 if you are making your own piping. Place the raw edge of the piping seam allowance along the right side of the curved edge of the bill. If needed, clip the piping seam allowance to facilitate following the curve. Stitch the piping to the curved edge of the bill along the seamline (**FIG. 4**).

10 Align the second layer of the flannel (bill lining) with the piped bill right sides together. Stitch

the seam on the curved edge only (**FIG. 5**). Trim the seam allowance and clip along curves. Turn and press with the piping extending from the seam edge.

11 With blue thread, hand whip the picot trim under the blue piping (**FIG. 6**).

12 Pin the bill to the bonnet with the right sides together centering the bill to the cap front edge. Pin the blue lining to the cap with right sides together; the bill should be sandwiched between the layers. Stitch the seam all around leaving

a 2" (5 cm) opening along the back neck edge (**FIG. 7**). Turn the lining to the inside though the opening and press the seams.

13 Cut ⅝" (1.5 cm) silk satin ribbon in half to make two ties. Fold a triple-loop bow in a shifted stack, as shown in the drawing, and stitch down the center of the bow leaving an 8" (20.5 cm) thread tail (**FIG. 8**). Gather the bow and secure it to the cap corner by hand, using the thread tail (pull the center loop up and tack-stitch to hold it upright.

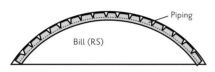

Piping

Bill (RS)

FIGURE 4

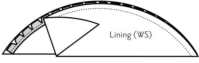

Lining (WS)

FIGURE 5

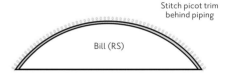

Stitch picot trim behind piping

Bill (RS)

FIGURE 6

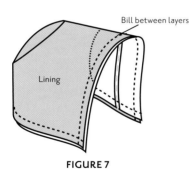

Bill between layers

Lining

FIGURE 7

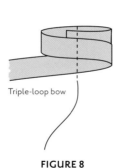

Triple-loop bow

FIGURE 8

Baby John Booties Construction

1. Stitch a machine eyelet or tiny buttonhole in the center front of both lining and bootie pieces so when they align, a ribbon tie can be threaded through both layers.

2. Stitch the back seam of the flannel shoe. Stitch the back seam of the blue shoe lining.

3. Place the blue shoe lining to the flannel shoe with right sides together, and stitch the upper edge only **(FIG. 9)**. Turn the right side out and press the seam. With a needle and blue thread, hand whip the blue picot trim to the finished lining seam edge.

4. With a 1.5 stitch length, stay-stitch around the bottom edge of the shoe, joining the lining and flannel layers. Clip the seam to the stitching along the back curve (this will help shape the shoe to the sole).

5. Layer together the two flannel soles (one is for interlining). Hand-baste the sole to the shoe with right sides together treating the double-layered sole as one. Machine stitch to complete the seam **(FIG. 10)**.

6. With a 1.5 stitch length, stay-stitch around the edge of the blue sole lining **(FIG. 11)**. Press the seam allowance to the inside. Place the wrong side of the lining on the inside bootie sole and hand whip around the edges to enclose the sole seams **(FIG. 12)**. Turn right side out.

7. Fold the shoe cuff down to the right side of the bootie along the foldline indicated on the pattern.

8. Cut two 17" (43 cm) pieces of ¼" (6 mm) ribbon for ties. Place the ribbon under the cuff and thread the ends through the eyelet at the center front **(FIG. 13)**. Center the ribbon on the back shoe seam. Straight-stitch in the ditch of the cuff seam to tack down the ribbon and cuff (the ribbon will be hidden under the cuff) **(FIG. 14)**.

9. Tack-stitch the front cuff edges to secure to the shoe **(FIG. 15)**.

10. Place the bootie on the baby's foot; pull the ribbon to fit and tie a bow.

FIGURE 9

FIGURE 10

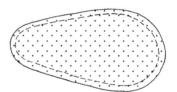

FIGURE 11

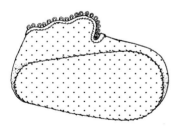

FIGURE 12

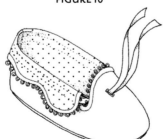

FIGURE 13

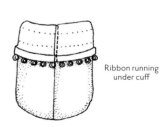

FIGURE 14

Ribbon running under cuff

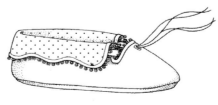

FIGURE 15

À la Boutis Provençal Bonnet

by Marie Yolande

BOUTIS PROVENÇAL IS PRIMARILY PRACTICED IN FRANCE in areas of Provence and Marseille. Although the technique may look intricate, it is actually quite easy to execute with a few basic tools and materials. In short, it is a padding technique, but differs from both trapunto and quilting. Traditionally for trapunto, the back fabric layer is slit open for the insertion of small pieces of stuffing, then the slits are hand-stitched closed. Boutis work involves stitching a design onto two layers of fabric with nothing between. This creates narrow channels between the stitching lines. Yarn is inserted into the channels with a large, long needle through the bottom fabric layer. This creates the raised, dimensional texture on the right side. Holes created by the needle close naturally when laundered. The pattern for our featured boutis piece, an adorable bonnet designed by Marie Yolande, can be found on the CD-rom, and her technique for executing boutis are on the following pages.

What You'll Need...

PATTERN

(available on the CD-rom)

"Boutis Bonnet with Boutis Design"

FABRIC

Two pieces of white cotton boutis batiste 21" × 16" (53.5 × 40.5 cm)

TRIM

½ yd (45.5 cm) of Swiss edging strip with a ¾" (2 cm) embroidered width

¾ yd (68.5 cm) of scalloped and Swiss edging with a ¼" (23 cm) embroidered width

1 yd (91.5 cm) of white double-face silk ribbon ⅝" (1.5 cm) wide

THREADS

¾ yd (68.5 cm) white cotton string (for cinching back of bonnet)

White cotton sewing thread, quilting thread or cotton/poly thread

Lightweight (60/2) basting thread in contrast color

Light color and weight basting thread 60/2

Loose-twist four-ply white cotton yarn (for stuffing)

TOOLS

#7 between needle (for stitching the marked lines)

#1 straw/milliner's needle (for sculpting cut yarn inside motifs)

#16 tapestry needle (to stuff small motifs and cord short channels)

5" (12.5 cm) long weaving/tapestry needle (to stuff large motifs and cord long channels)

Two round toothpicks

SUPPLIES

Wash-away mechanical pencil (such as the Ultimate Marking Pencil for Quilters and Crafters)

Wooden embroidery hoop with an adjustable screw 4"–6" (10–15 cm) (preferably with center hoop wrapped with a strip of cotton batiste)

Masking tape

Grid ruler

Pins

Thimble

Pattern tracing paper

Sharp scissors

Mild laundry soap: Ivory, Savon de Marseille, Biz, or Oxi Clean

Soft bristle toothbrush

NOTE: For additional boutis patterns that coordinate with this bonnet, contact Marie Yolande. Consult the Contributor's page 141.

Boutis work is considered an embroidery technique. Categorized as a raised cording technique, it requires neither batting nor cutting of fabric to achieve the sculptural effects and is totally reversible. Two unwashed fabric layers are sewn together using both running and backstitches to create the designs and channels before stuffing is inserted. The stuffing is executed with a large tapestry needle, which is threaded with cotton yarn and inserted between the fabric fibers in the top (bottom) layer of the stitched motifs and channels. During this process, the holes left by the large tapestry needle can be "combed" closed with the aid of a wooden toothpick. Because the fabric is not prewashed, the holes completely close and disappear during laundering. Depending on the fabric, amount of stuffing and cording, the shrinking rate of a boutis item can range between 7 and 13 percent. Pattern pieces for the use of the boutis technique are graded accordingly.

Patterns and design for the collection shown are included in the project booklet *Baby Layette à la Boutis Provençal* by Marie Yolande (see resources).

How to Make It...

Preparation

1 Tape the pattern pieces to a flat surface.

2 Iron the batiste pieces to remove any obvious wrinkles. Do not use starch, heavy steam, or prewash fabric. NOTE: *The creases will disappear in washing and a completed boutis never needs ironing; the puckered appearance is a desired design element.* Set one of the batiste pieces aside.

3 Fold the remaining piece of fabric in half in the direction of the grain line and use your finger to crease the folded edge. Unfold and center the fabric over the bonnet pattern. While referring to the grain-line markings, pin or tape in place as you individually mark each section; reposition the batiste to trace all three pieces. A space of 1¼" (3.2 cm) between the pattern pieces is required for seam allowances, and a sufficient amount of room on the outside edges is necessary to position the fabric in an embroidery hoop.

4 Working from the center out, trace all the marked lines shown on the pattern with a fine-point lead fabric pencil. Use a ruler to draw the lines and avoid dragging your pencil over the long distances on the fabric as it may distort the design. Lift the pencil every 2" (5 cm) or so while marking the batiste (**FIG. 1**).

5 After all the markings have been transferred, place the marked batiste on top of the second piece of white fabric while matching the grain lines. Pin and baste the two layers together in a grid pattern every 2" (2.5 cm) with a light color thread. Avoid basting directly on the marked design lines. Remove the pins (**FIG. 2**).

Stitching

1 Position the basted fabric layers in an embroidery hoop. The fabric should be stretched taut with some flexibility to allow for a running stitch.

2 Thread #7 between needle with one strand of white sewing thread about 15" (38 cm) long; knot the end of a single strand. Thread is red in photo for best visibility.

3 Insert the needle through the top marked layer of fabric about 1" (2.5 cm) or more from the starting point (anywhere in the open area is fine). Bring the needle up next to the start of a stitching line where the marked lines intersect. To hide the knot, pull on the thread until the knot pops through and is between the two layers of fabric next to the starting point.

4 Make a short backstitch before beginning the running stitch to stabilize the thread. Continue to stitch on the marked line with running stitches through both layers (**FIG. 3**, front view, and **FIG. 4**, back view). NOTE: *Although you may strive for stitching perfection, your running stitches do not have to be perfectly even. The stitching line will be located in the valleys of the raised designs, and the fabric will shrink along with the thread when laundered.*

5 End each stitching line with one or two short backstitches and travel with your threaded needle between the fabric layers along a marked line. Do not travel across the center of a motif. Doing so will interfere with the cording procedure. Exit about an inch (2.5 cm) away and clip the thread. This will hide the tail thread inside the motif and between the layers.

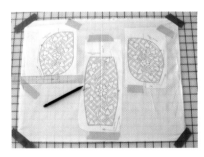

FIGURE 1

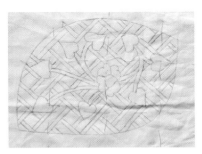

FIGURE 2

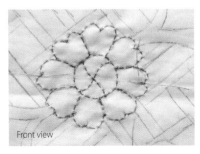

Front view

FIGURE 3

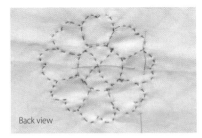

Back view

FIGURE 4

FIGURE 5

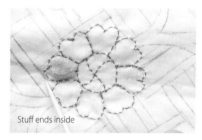

FIGURE 6

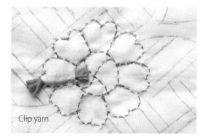

FIGURE 7

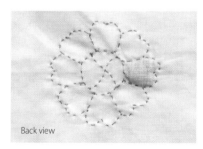

FIGURE 8

6 Complete all stitching and remove all basting threads before starting on the cording and stuffing.

Stuffing

Work from the center out in this order: First, stuff the flower and heart motifs, then stems, and finally the channels on the trellis frame.

1 Thread a #16 tapestry needle with white cotton yarn about 20" (51 cm) long. Red yarn is used in the photos for best visibility. Fold the strand in half until the tail ends are even.

2 Insert the needle through the top layer of a stitched design and travel between the fabric layers. Bring the needle up at the opposite end of the motif while positioning the yarn and fabric between your index finger and thumb. Doing so will both release stress on the open fabric fibers and guide the yarn through the hole while preventing the strands from becoming twisted (**FIG. 5**).

3 Cut the yarn about ⅛" (3 mm) from the exit point (**FIG. 6**).

4 Insert the point of an unthreaded #1 straw/milliner's needle into the center of the top fabric layer; work the needle tip between the layers to catch the yarn and pull the tail ends of the yarn inside. Use the tip of the needle to shift the yarn inside the layers to spread it evenly.

5 Repeat to stuff more yarn into the motif until the desired density is achieved. In this instance, avoid over-stuffing a motif because it may be uncomfortable for a newborn baby to lie on excessively raised designs. Do not insert the threaded tapestry needle in the same hole more than three times as it may damage the fibers, causing a permanent hole. Sculpt the motifs to your liking with #1 straw needle.

6 Close the holes with a wooden toothpick by combing the point of a toothpick in the direction that the fibers are woven both lengthwise (warp) and crosswise (weft) (**FIG. 7**, front view, and **FIG. 8**, back view). These openings will also mend naturally when the project is laundered in the last step.

Cording

After completing all the flowers and heart motifs, proceed to the cording stems and channels found on the trellis.

1 Thread a 5" (12.5 cm) long tapestry needle with one strand of white cotton yarn about 20" (51 cm) long. Fold the strand in half until the tail ends are even.

2 Insert the needle at the starting point of a stem, travel between the layers and come up at the end (**FIG. 9**). Clip and stuff as you did before for the shaped sections. For long channels, it may be possible for the tail ends of the yarn to pop inside the channels by holding one end very firmly and pulling on the fabric at the opposite end.

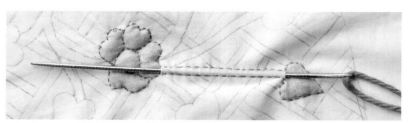

FIGURE 9

Hand Laundering

After all stitching, stuffing, and cording have been completed, soak your boutis piece in clear, tepid water for a few minutes and drain the water. This will start the shrinking process and remove some of the obvious lead markings. Fill a separate basin or tub with warm water and dissolve in it a soap product such as Savon de Marseille Soap from Marseille, Oxi Clean, Ivory, or Biz. Do not use any bleaching agents. Immerse the boutis project along with the embroidery strips in soapy water and allow them to soak overnight. Gently scrub any remaining markings with a soft bristle toothbrush, adding soap to the bristles as necessary. NOTE: *The lead markings will appear darker when wet; after the bonnet is assembled, wash again to remove any remaining marks.* Rinse well until all the soap residue is gone. Roll the wet boutis piece in a clean, absorbent white towel, and then unroll and place the wet boutis to dry on a sweater rack. Do not squeeze the boutis as you may permanently flatten some of the stuffed motifs and destroy the puckered appearance, which is characteristic of boutis embroidery.

FIGURE 10

Cutting Seam Allowances

1 When the boutis is completely dry, place it flat on a cutting table. Because some shrinkage inevitably occurs during laundering, the seam allowance areas will look ruffled.

2 From the corded edge of a boutis piece, measure and mark a ½" (1.3 cm) seam allowance around all three sections of the bonnet.

3 Mark the pattern notches with colored thread on the wrong side (this was the side that was marked) using a tailor's tack, knot, and clip the tails.

4 Cut on the marked seam allowances and place all three sections with thread tacks showing on the top **(FIG. 10)**.

Assembling the Bonnet

1 Pin the center section and one side section together. The stitched loops will identify the locations of the notches inside of the bonnet. Make certain that the overall design of the flower and hearts on the side section of the bonnet are pointing upward.

2 Thread a #7 between needle with white sewing thread and make a knot at the end of a single strand.

3 Hand-baste the seam: At the start of the seamline, go through all four layers of the seam allowances in a stabbing motion and make a long running stitch about ¼" (6 mm) long. Continue piecing the sections together with an in-and-out stabbing motion and end the seam with a couple of backstitches. Insert the tail end of the thread between the fabric layers in a corded area.

4 With a new piece of thread, sew the seam by hand with backstitches: Make a row of short backstitches on top of the existing row of long running stitches and sightly add tension on the thread when reaching the crown area. Doing so will help shape the bonnet in a rounded manner to fit the contour of a baby's head.

5 Finish the seam by concealing the tail end of the thread in a corded area between the fabric layers.

6 Pin and seam the other side of the bonnet to the center section in the same manner.

7 Clip away the tack stitches making the notches.

Seam Finishing

1 Grade the seam allowance: Trim away the underneath side of the seam allowances to ⅛" (3 mm) wide, leaving remaining seam allowance untrimmed.

2 Fold the raw edge of the remaining seam allowance under once and then over the cut seam allowance so that the cut seam allowance is enclosed. Pin and stitch by hand with a blind stitch. This creates a ¼" (6 mm) bound seam.

3 Finish the remaining seams in this manner.

Finishing the Outside Edge of the Bonnet

1 Trim away the inside edge of the seam allowance to ⅛" (3 mm) wide all around the bonnet, grading it in the same manner as for the seams.

2 Fold the top layer of the seam allowance in half toward the inside of the bonnet.

3 Pin the ¼" (6 mm) wide seam allowance and blind-stitch or whipstitch into place with one strand of white sewing thread.

4 Wash the bonnet by following the laundering instructions at left.

Joining the Swiss Trim

1 From the back side of the Swiss trim, steam press and if necessary, use starch or sizing for a crisp finish.

2 Cut an 18" (45.5 cm) long strip from the wider edging trim and set aside for the making of the rosettes.

3 Trim away the seam allowances to the remaining strips next to the row of entredeux.

4 From the back side, whipstitch the wide and narrow edgings together with fine heirloom embroidery thread.

5 As you stitch, gather the wider embroidery strip to the narrow one to create a ruffled effect.

Attaching the Embroidery Strip to the Bonnet

1 From the inside center back of the bonnet, butt and pin the gathered Swiss edging strip to the folded edge.

2 With one strand of fine white heirloom thread knotted at one end, whipstitch the edging to the edge of the bonnet by taking a stitch into the folded seam and connect the strip by stitching into the entredeux openings. Start stitching 1" (2.5 cm) from the tail end of the strip. Continue all around the bonnet until you arrive at the starting point.

3 To join the ends without a seam, overlap the embroidered motifs on the strip and whipstitch the motifs with fine thread around the outline of the motif shape. Finish attaching the strip to the bonnet.

4 Thread a 16# tapestry needle with the white string and starting at the center lower back of the bonnet, weave a single strand of the string in and out of the eyelets found on the narrow embroidery strip. From both tail ends of the string, pull slightly to shape the bonnet. Tie both ends of the string with a knot and a bow.

Making the Side Rosettes

1 Fold the 18" (45.5 cm) Swiss edging in half and cut. Set one 9" (23 cm) strip aside.

2 By hand, with a single strand of white sewing thread, French seam the cut ends to encase the raw seam allowances and form a circle of trim. Refer to French Seam in the Techniques section on page 124 if needed.

3 Thread a #7 needle with white sewing thread and knot the tail ends together.

4 Run a gathering stitch in the ring of trim: From the back, at about ½" (1.3 cm) from the cut seam, secure the thread with a backstitch. Stitch a row of running stitches all around the circle. Pull the thread to gather and form the rosette. Secure with a couple of backstitches to lock gathering.

5 Clip one strand of the thread tail and leave the remaining strand to attach the rosette to the side of the bonnet.

Attaching the Rosettes and Ribbon to Sides of the Bonnet

1 On the lower corner of the bonnet, attach the rosettes and stitch into place.

2 At ¾" (2 cm) from the end of a ribbon tail, fold the ribbon to form a loop. Stitch across with two strands of white sewing thread, pinch together with thumb and index finger, wrap thread around the gathered section.

3 Stitch through in a stabbing manner, backstitch to secure the thread and cut one strand.

4 Fold back the ribbon loop onto itself over the gathered section to conceal the stitches.

5 With the remaining strand of thread, stitch the inside edge of the loop to form a raised, rounded bubble and attach it to the center of the rosette while covering the gathered line of the rosette. Repeat on the other side of the bonnet.

Fancy Ribbon Sash Baby Bibs

BY LAURA JENKINS THOMPSON

V & A images/Victoria & Albert Museum

THE CONTINENTAL BIB from the *Victoria & Albert Museum of Childhood* book is just the elegant style baby needs to protect a precious gown worn beneath. Based on an antique from her vintage collection, Laura Jenkins Thompson's bib (page 108) is similar in feel and hails from the same era. We've provided both bib patterns on the CD-rom along with a bonus butterfly machine shadow-stitch embroidery download, a hand-embroidery bluebird template, and the floral spray template from the Continental design. The instructions for making Laura's bib, which is self-lined and finished around the edge with straight lace and pin stitching, and directions for stitching out the butterfly embroidery designs are detailed in this chapter.

What You'll Need...

PATTERN
(available on the CD-rom)

"Fancy Ribbon Sash Bib"

"Continental Bib"

FABRIC & TRIM

⅓ yd (30.5 cm) of white handkerchief linen or batiste

2 yd (1.8 m) of ⅝" wide (1.5 cm) lace edging

EMBROIDERY
(available on the CD-rom)

"Butterfly" shadow embroidery by machine design (sized for 4 × 4 hoop)

"Bluebird of Happiness" shadow embroidery handwork design

Floral spray handwork template

SUPPLIES

#120 jeans needle for pinstitching

#70 embroidery or Metafil needle

One ½"–⅝" (1.3–1.5 cm) pearl shank button

24" (61 cm) of ¾" (2 cm) wide silk satin ribbon

DMC Six-strand embroidery floss (to hand-shadow-stitch bluebird)

  #225 ultra v lt shell pink

  #368 v lt pistachio green

  #828 v lt blue

Robison-Anton Machine Embroidery Thread (to machine shadow-stitch butterfly)

  #2206 baby blue

  #2414 coral

  #2234 glow

  #2230 tamarack

  #2434 tropic blue

White fine machine sewing thread

Water-soluble stabilizer

Temporary spray adhesive

Blue wash-away marking pen

Hand-embroidery hoop (optional)

What to Cut...

FROM MAIN FABRIC

Square for bib front large enough to hoop

How to Make It...

Machine Shadow Embroidery

1 Spray starch and press fabric.

2 Using a wash-away marking pen, trace the bib pattern to prepared fabric. Mark where you would like the butterfly centered on the bib. Do not cut out.

3 Adhere two layers of water-soluble stabilizer together with temporary spray adhesive and hoop. Mark the hoop's center on the top stabilizer layer with a wash-away marking pen.

4 Wind the bobbin with white thread.

5 Using a #70 needle, Robinson-Anton thread colors listed and stitching directly on the stabilizer, follow the embroidery sequence stitch order on the CD-rom (colors 1–4).

6 When you reach the sequence that says "place and center fabric in hoop," remove the hoop from the machine and apply temporary spray adhesive directly to the area to be stitched and lightly to the back of the square of fabric to which you've traced the bib. Match the center of the stitched-out design to the mark you made in Step 2 to center the butterfly on the bib. Smooth out the fabric but do not stretch.

7 Return the hoop to the machine and continue the embroidery sequences to completion (**FIG. 1**).

8 When the embroidery has been completed, remove your project from the hoop. Cut away the larger portions of the stabilizer from the embroidery on the back (**FIG. 2**).

FIGURE 1

FIGURE 2

Soak and rinse the remaining stabilizer and center markings from the fabric. Let dry and press the finished embroidery on a folded towel. Retrace the bib pattern to the fabric square positioning the butterfly as desired.

NOTE: *If you would prefer to hand-shadow-stitch the bluebird or hand-embroider the floral spray on your bib, trace the bib pattern to a fabric square large enough to secure in a hand-embroidery hoop. Trace off the chosen design and follow the embroidery or shadow-work instructions, if necessary, which can be found in the Techniques section on page 124.*

Bib Construction

1 Thread machine with white fine sewing thread.

2 Cut another square of linen the same size as the embroidered bib square to serve as the lining.

3 Place lining square beneath machine embroidered bib front square with wrong sides together and right side of embroidery facing up. Baste together carefully along stitching lines using a straight stitch **(FIG. 3)**. Cut out bib ¾"–1" (2–2.5 cm) from stitching line.

4 On a shaping board or ironing board, shape lace around entire perimeter of bib starting at one shoulder corner. Pin along scalloped edge, while aligning lace heading along machine-stitched basting lines.

5 Pull lace heading thread to ease lace into shape along curves; miter pointed edges **(FIG. 4)**. Re-pin lace flat to fabric.

6 Baste lace edging along header edge using a zigzag (L=1.5; W=1.5).

7 Spray starch and press. Clip fabric under lace along curves and press fabric back away from lace on to bib.

8 Change needle to a #100-120 jeans needle.

9 Change machine setting to pinstitch with length and width (about L=2.0; W=2.5). (Test before actually stitching.) Mirror image if necessary so that the vertical stitch will be on the fabric and the horizontal stitches will be only on the lace.

10 Pinstitch lace along entire bib edge.

11 On wrong side of bib, trim away raw edges close to stitching line **(FIG. 5)**.

12 Position button and buttonhole. Stitch buttonhole in place by machine.

13 Trim away excess stabilizer. Soak bib in clear water, let dry, and iron.

14 Cut length of silk ribbon in half. Fold back raw edges and stitch in place on both sides by hand **(FIG. 6)**.

15 Stitch shank button in place by hand.

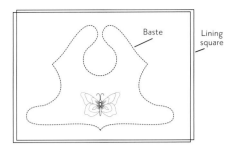

FIGURE 3

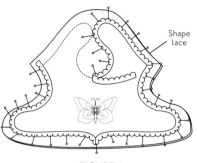

FIGURE 4

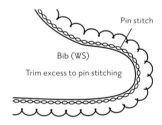

FIGURE 5

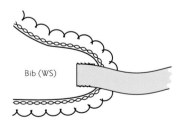

FIGURE 6

Baby Chick Coverlet

BY WENDY POCHE SCHOEN

THIS PRECIOUS COVERLET FEATURES ultra-soft, puffy appliquéd chicks delicately arranged around the edges. This easy technique involves making little "pillows" of machine-stitched and stuffed appliqués of soft stretch terrycloth, which are hand appliquéd onto the base fabric then embroidered with imported wool embroidery. The base of the coverlet is imported cotton sateen, quilted by hand in the tradition of Sashiko* then further embellished with wool embroidery. The coverlet is interlined with soft flannel fabric and bordered with a large scalloped flange.

What You'll Need...

PATTERN
(available on the CD-rom)

Duck template

Embroidery design

Scallop border and corner patterns

FABRIC

1 yd (91.5 cm) of 60" (152.5 cm) wide white cotton sateen

1⅔ yd (152.5 cm) of 60" (152.5 cm) wide yellow cotton sateen

1⅔ yd (152.5 cm) of 45" (114.5 cm) wide white cotton flannel

½ yd (23 cm) of yellow terrycloth

SUPPLIES

Wet N Gone Fusible stabilizer

Appleton Wool Thread (See Color Key)

Spool of Sulky #12, Light Yellow

Polyester fiber filling for stuffing chicks

Embroidery needles:

#24 chenille

#8 crewel

#1 milliner

#10 sharp

Spool of white Coats Extra-Fine Thread

Spool of white polyester thread

18" or 24" (45.5 or 61 cm) quilting ruler

Crewel needle threader

Purple Thang™

Fine-point blue wash-away marking pen

6" (15 cm) hand-embroidery hoop

Sewing machine feet

Clear plastic

Appliqué

Embroidery scissors

Dressmaker shears

Straight pins

COLOR KEY
APPLETON WOOL

	541 Green
	551 Yellow
	751 Lt. Pink
	753 Med. Pink
	861 Orange
	891 Lt. Lavender
	892 Med. Lavender
	991B White

What to Cut and Prep...

Refer to cutting diagrams on CD-rom for each fabric.

FROM WHITE COTTON SATEEN

NOTE: *Spritz the blocks of flannel and cotton sateen with water, spray starch, then iron dry before cutting.*

39" (L) × 31" (W) (99 × 79 cm) scalloped border pieces

FROM WHITE FLANNEL

39" (L) × 31" (W) (99 × 79 cm)

NOTE: *Lining for four corner pieces and scallop pieces will be cut out in a later step.*

FROM YELLOW TERRYCLOTH

Two 7" × 9" (18 × 23 cm) pieces for ducks

FROM YELLOW COTTON SATEEN

NOTE: *Spritz the yellow cotton with water, spray starch, and iron it dry.*

Two 7" × 9" (18 × 23 cm) pieces for ducks

FROM WET N GONE FUSIBLE

Four 7" × 9" (18 × 23 cm) pieces for ducks

PREPPING SCALLOPED BORDER

Spritz the yellow cotton sateen with water, spray starch, and iron it dry.

Transfer the fourteen full scallop shapes with quilting lines and the four corners on the right side with a blue wash-away marking pen; leave a bit of space between the shapes.

Rough cut all of the scallop pieces out in block form to separate the shapes but do not cut on the pattern lines.

Cut the blocks of flannel the same size to back each of the scallops and corners. Spritz each flannel block with water, and iron dry. Set the blocks aside for now.

How to Make It...

Sashiko is a very old form of hand sewing using a simple running stitch sewn in repeating or interlocking patterns through one or more layers of fabric. Originally designed for quilting together several layers of fabric for warmth and durability or for strengthening a single layer of fabric, Sashiko patterns readily lend themselves to contemporary designs and projects. NOTE: *The Babylock Sashiko machine is a modern-day alternative to working Sashiko by hand.*

Coverlet Front

1 On the white cotton sateen right side, center and transfer the entire embroidery template with a fine-point blue wash-away marking pen. NOTE: *If you find the fabric is too heavy to see through, transfer the design onto the Wet N Gone Tacky and then affix it onto the right side of the cotton sateen. After embroidering, just wash the Wet N Gone away.* Pin the flannel to the wrong side of the cotton sateen and baste it in place securely all around from center out (**FIG. 1**). Beginning at the center, stitch straight through the horizontal center of the coverlet. Stitch across the coverlet in the opposite direction from the center. Repeat in the vertical direction, then baste diagonally from corner to corner in both directions.

2 Quilt the crisscross lines in the center of the coverlet with a single strand of yellow Sulky #12, a #7 between needle, and even running stitches.

3 Position the appliqués (see appliqué instructions below) to the coverlet top and pin in place. Blindstitch the appliqués to the coverlet with polyester thread.

4 Complete the hand embroidery entirely. (The embroidery design is available on the CD-rom and the stitch diagrams can be found in the Techniques section on page 124).

Making the Appliqués

1 Trace the four chicks onto the non-adhesive side of the Wet N Gone Fusible stabilizer with a blue wash-away marking pen, using the provided templates.

2 Position the adhesive side of the stabilizer to the RIGHT side of the yellow terrycloth squares. (You should be able to fit two chicks in each square, leaving two for a future project.) Fuse the stabilizer using a pressing cloth and hot iron (**FIG. 2**).

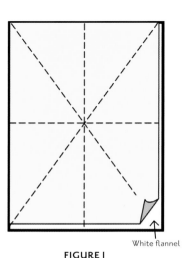

FIGURE I

White flannel

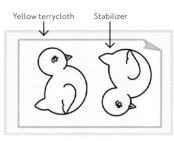

Yellow terrycloth   Stabilizer

FIGURE 2

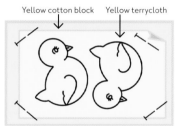

Yellow cotton block   Yellow terrycloth

FIGURE 3

3 Place the terrycloth blocks to the yellow cotton blocks right sides together. Pin securely in place (**FIG. 3**).

4 Sew around the OUTER edges of each chick with the lightening stitch. This stitch looks like a little lightning bolt on your machine directory (L=1.5; W=1.5).

5 Cut out the chicks, cutting very close to the lightening stitch (**FIG. 4**). Cut a slit through the cotton at the center of the chick.

6 Turn the appliqué right sides out and using a skewer or Purple Thang™, smooth all the seams.

7 Using very small amounts, begin stuffing the appliqué through the slit until it puffs up slightly. Do not overstuff the appliqué. Sew the slit closed by hand with a herringbone stitch (**FIG. 5**).

Stitching the Appliqués

1 Position the chick onto the coverlet and couch in place with long random stitches, "Gulliver style" (**FIG. 6**). (These stitches will be removed later.)

2 With a single strand of Coats sewing thread and #10 sharp needle, position two backstitches beneath the appliqué to tie on.

3 Working in a hoop, emerge from beneath. Sew up through the fabric and just catch the edge of the appliqué, sewing through the cotton fabric only (**FIG. 7**).

4 Holding the needle perpendicular to the fabric and just beside the appliqué, sew through the coverlet to the back; tighten.

5 Place the next stitch about ¼" (6 mm) away and repeat the process until the stitches go completely around the appliqué. Remove the holding stitches.

6 Backstitch the interior lines such as the wing with one strand of yellow wool in a chenille needle.

7 Stitch the eye in a granito stitch; outline the beak in a stem stitch with straight satin stitches inside the foundation (orange), and work the feet in straight stitch.

Stitching the Scallops

1 Stitch the right corner section to the left corner section, right sides together, to form the corner scallops (**FIGS. 8 AND 9**). Once stitched, treat as one.

2 Back the fourteen full scallop shapes and the four corner scallops with cotton flannel, pinning together. Baste the scallops to the flannel securely then remove the pins (**SEE FIG. 9**). Quilt along the interior lines of each scallop and the corners with a single strand of yellow Sulky #12 and the #7 between needle.

3 Tie on with a small backstitch on the back.

4 Beginning with the scallops, work a very small, evenly spaced running stitch directly on the design line (**FIG. 10**). The stitch length should be no less than eight or ten stitches per inch and worked without an embroidery hoop. Repeat for the corners.

5 Stay-stitch along the seamlines of all the scallops (L=2.5). This step provides a guideline when applying the facings.

FIGURE 4

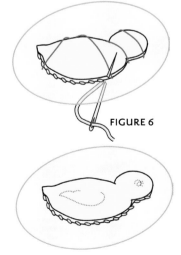

FIGURE 6

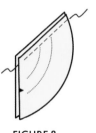

FIGURE 8

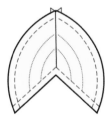

FIGURE 9

FIGURE 5

FIGURE 7

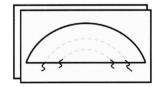

FIGURE 10

6 Apply the facing pieces to the scallops, right sides together. Stitch the curved edge of each scallop (L=2.5) through all thicknesses, using the stay-stitching to guide your stitching (**FIG. 11**).

7 To face the corners, seam together the corner facing pieces of the right and left sections, then with right sides together (**SEE FIGS. 8 AND 9**). Pin the corner facing to the corner piece right sides together, aligning the seams. Sew the curved edge along the stay-stitching line.

8 Cut out the scallops a scant ¼" (6 cm) from the stitching. Trim the flannel very close to the stitching to reduce the bulk, clip the curves, and turn right sides out (**FIG. 12**). Press the seams well; baste the open edge closed (**FIG. 13**).

Attaching the Edging

1 Measure the coverlet top carefully, then trim the fabric evenly and exactly to the required measurement of 32" wide × 39" long (79 × 99 cm).

2 On the outside with right sides together, pin the corner scallops to the coverlet top, aligning the edges evenly (**FIG. 14**).

3 Position the scallops around the edges of the coverlet, adjusting the spacing as necessary.

4 Stitch around all the edges. Trim and grade the seams; clip as necessary.

Backing

1 Starch and iron the yellow cotton sateen rectangle.

2 Beginning at the top edge of the coverlet, pin the backing fabric in place having right sides together and aligning corners, edges, and grainlines (**FIG. 15**).

3 Sew the backing to the coverlet, leaving a 12" (30.5 cm) area for turning. Turn right sides out (**SEE FIG. 15**).

4 Re-align the scallops and then press the edges well. Slip-stitch the opening closed.

5 Through all layers, stitch a stitch border inside the edges of the coverlet <u>matching the quilting stitches</u> of the main design (**FIG. 16**).

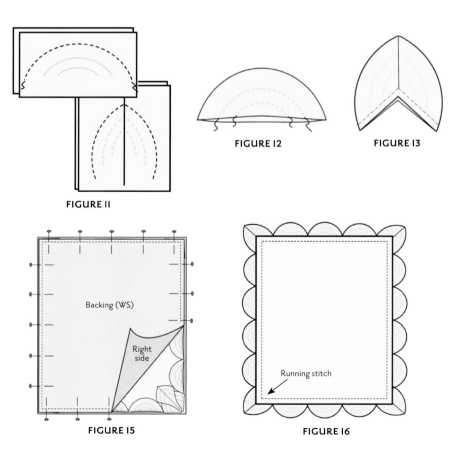

FIGURE 11

FIGURE 12

FIGURE 13

FIGURE 14

FIGURE 15

Backing (WS)

Right side

FIGURE 16

Running stitch

Christening Accessories Holder

Alternative Vintage Royal Alphabet for machine embroidery can be found on the CD-rom.

A CHRISTENING ACCESSORIES HOLDER IS THE PERFECT WAY to store christening accessories that were part of a baby's important ceremony. It will protect those adorable socks, a bonnet, tiny jewelry, and other items that will carry meaning through a lifetime. The pocketed holder is secured over a padded hanger, so you can tuck your memories away and hang them wherever you hang your gown. This project can also be enlarged to fit an adult hanger, if desired. The front and back of the accessories holder each have three zippered pockets. An optional monogram may be added to the middle or lower pocket of the front to personalize it. Each pocket front is lined to totally enclose the zipper tape. The pictured holder is made from white cotton sateen with ecru embroidery and embellishments. Change out the ecru to white for an equally beautiful project.

What You'll Need...

PATTERN
(available on the CD-rom)

Hanger curved template

Corner template

FABRIC

1⅓ yd (124.5 cm) of 54" (137 cm) wide white cotton sateen

TRIM

3¼ yd (297.5 cm) of ¼" (6 mm) wide white or ecru silk satin ribbon

EMBROIDERY
(available on the CD-rom)

Vintage Royal Alphabet Machine Embroidery Collection

SUPPLIES

Four 14" (35.5 cm) nylon zippers, white or ecru

One 12" (30.5 cm) child's padded hanger

Floriani Perfect Stick Stabilizer, 8" × 10" (20.5 × 25.5 cm)

One small spool of white or ecru 60 wt Mettler thread for embroidery

White bobbin thread

White 50 wt sewing thread for construction

Roxanne's Glue Baste-It

Fabric folding pen

Quilting ruler

Size 75 embroidery needle for embroidery and construction

Blue wash-away marking pen

Rotary cutter, ruler, and mat

Glass-head pins

EMBROIDERY DESIGN

The machine monogram design on the sample project shown is from *Creative Monogram Software* by Martha Pullen Company, Font: Wedded Bliss; Style: Mono 3 Letter Center; Size: 2.49" high × 5.10" wide (6.5 × 12.5 cm).

For an alternative machine embroidery design, the complete *Vintage Royal Alphabet* is available on the CD-rom.

What to Cut...

(cutting guide on the CD-rom)

FROM THE COTTON SATEEN

Twelve rectangles, 7½" × 12" (19 × 30.5 cm) to create the holder front

Two rectangles, 22½" × 12" (57 × 30.5 cm) for the lining

How to Make It...

Please read through directions before beginning. Be sure to use a fabric press cloth when pressing the holder fabric to avoid scorching starch or transferring iron residue to the fabric.

Embroidery

1 Choose one 7½" × 12" (19 × 30.5 cm) rectangle. Spray starch and press the fabric. Fold the piece into quarters and mark the vertical and horizontal center.

2 Choose a monogram design and load the design into your machine. Hoop a piece of Floriani Perfect Stick Stabilizer paper side up. Score and remove the paper inside the hoop. Mark the center of the stabilizer.

3 Adhere the fabric rectangle to the stabilizer matching the centers. Hand press the fabric to the stabilizer.

4 Embroider the monogram. Remove the fabric from the hoop and carefully tear away the stabilizer.

5 Spray the blue marks with water. Allow to dry to ensure blue marks do not return. Spray the piece again and while the piece is still damp, place the fabric right side down on a fluffy towel. Press the fabric from the back until dry.

Creating the Accessories Holder Front and Back

Seam allowances are ½" (1.3 cm) unless otherwise noted.

Back

1 Select two 7½" × 12" (19 × 30.5 cm) rectangles. Using a Fabric Folding Pen, mark a line ½" (1.3 cm) from the raw edge along both 12" (30.5 cm) sides of each piece. Fold ½" (1.3 cm) to the wrong side along each long edge (**FIG. 1**). Press.

2 Place one zipper right side up on a flat surface. Glue-baste the fold of the fabric to the zipper with the fold touching the zipper teeth. An equal amount of zipper should extend past the fabric on each side (**FIG. 2**). Finger press and allow to dry.

3 Flip the piece over and glue-baste the second fabric piece to the wrong side of the zipper. The fabrics should be wrong sides together, even at each side and even at the folds along the bottom edge. Finger press and allow to dry. Place a pin at each side through the fabric layers and zipper (**FIG. 3**).

4 Use a zipper foot or edge foot and adjust the needle position so you are stitching about ⅛" (3 mm) from the fold of the fabric and the zipper's edge. Stitch through the fabric and zipper (**FIG. 4**).

5 Select four 7½" × 12" (19 × 30.5 cm) rectangles. Using a fabric folding pen, mark a line ½" (1.3 cm) from the raw edge along ONE 12" (30.5 cm) side of each piece. Fold ½" (1.3 cm) to the wrong side along the long edge. Press.

6 Follow Steps 2–4 to attach the two rectangles above and two rectangles below the previously assembled piece. Be sure the sides of the fabric align (**FIG. 5A**).

Front

Repeat Steps 1–6 above to create the holder front using the embroidered rectangle for the lower or middle panel. Do not use the embroidered rectangle for the upper panel since this panel will be cut later to fit the hanger shape (**FIG. 5B**).

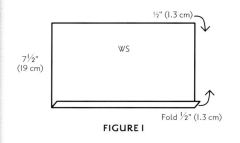

½" (1.3 cm)

7½" (19 cm)

WS

Fold ½" (1.3 cm)

FIGURE 1

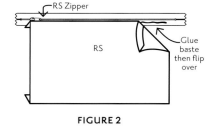

RS Zipper

RS

Glue baste then flip over

FIGURE 2

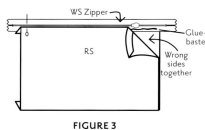

WS Zipper

RS

Glue-baste

Wrong sides together

FIGURE 3

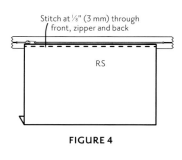

Stitch at ⅛" (3 mm) through front, zipper and back

RS

FIGURE 4

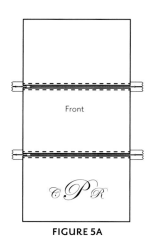

Front

𝒞𝒫ℛ

FIGURE 5A

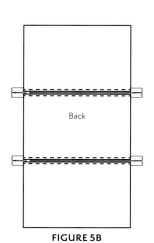

Back

FIGURE 5B

Preparing the Accessories Holder for Construction

1 Unzip each zipper to about 2" (5 cm) inside the fabric area. Pull the zipper together matching the zipper stops; bartack ⅜" (1 cm) inside the fabric edge **(FIG. 6)**. This will pull the zipper back together and prevent you from cutting away the zipper slide.

2 Bartack ⅜" (1 cm) inside the fabric edge at the end of each zipper **(SEE FIG. 6)**. This creates a new stop at the end of the zipper.

3 Place the holder back, right side down, on a flat surface. Place the two linings right sides together, and position them on the holder back. Place the holder front, right side up, on top of the backings. The linings should be slightly longer than the holder back and front **(FIG. 7)**.

4 Align the top and sides of all the layers. Pin all the layers together every 2" (5 cm) or so **(FIG. 8)**.

5 Using a ruler, mat, and rotary cutter, trim the linings even with the holder front and back. Also, cut away the excess zippers **(FIG. 9)**.

Important: Be sure the zipper slides are inside the fabric area of the holder.

6 Using the corner template, trim the lower two corners of all the layers **(FIG. 10)**.

7 Using the holder curve template, align the designated line on the template to the top edge of the layered fabrics. Trim all the layers at the top of the holder along the curved cutting line. Mark the two dots on one lining layer and the holder back **(FIG. 11)**.

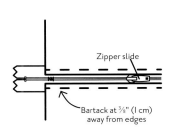

FIGURE 6

Zipper slide

Bartack at ⅜" (1 cm) away from edges

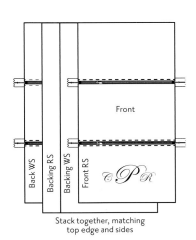

Front

Back WS | Backing RS | Backing WS | Front RS

Stack together, matching top edge and sides

FIGURE 7

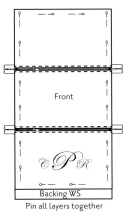

Front

Backing WS

Pin all layers together

FIGURE 8

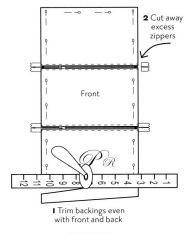

2 Cut away excess zippers

Front

1 Trim backings even with front and back

FIGURE 9

Using corner templates trim lower two corners of all layers

FIGURE 10

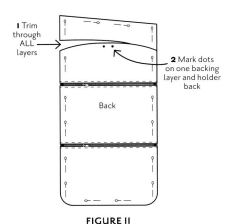

1 Trim through ALL layers

Back

2 Mark dots on one backing layer and holder back

FIGURE 11

Construction

1 Pin the holder front and holder back right sides together matching the top curved edges. Stitch a ½" (1.3 cm) seam, skipping the area between the dots. This will be the opening for the hanger hook. Be sure to backstitch at the dots to secure. Clip the seam allowance every ¼" (6 mm) or so **(FIG. 12)**. Press the seam open. Continue pressing the unstitched area open.

2 On each lining piece, individually stitch a "guideline" ½" (1.3 cm)

from the raw edge of the curve. The "guidelines" should be about 4" (10 cm) long and centered on the curve **(FIG. 13)**.

3 Pin the linings right sides together matching the top curved edges. Stitch a ½" (1.3 cm) seam, leaving 4" (10 cm) open in the center of the curve for turning. Clip the seam allowance every ¼" (6 mm) or so. Also clip the 4" (10 cm) area to the stitched guideline **(FIG. 14)**. Press the seam open. Continue pressing the unstitched area open folding along the stitched guideline.

4 Cut four 14" (35.5 cm) pieces of silk satin ribbon. Pin one end of each ribbon just above the uppermost zipper edge on the right side of the holder front and back. Match the raw edge of the ribbon to the raw edge of the holder. Fold the excess length of ribbon on each piece and pin to the center of the holder front and back **(FIG. 15)**. This will prevent the ribbon from accidentally being stitched in the seam.

5 Place the holder to the lining, right sides together, matching the raw edges. Straight-stitch all the way

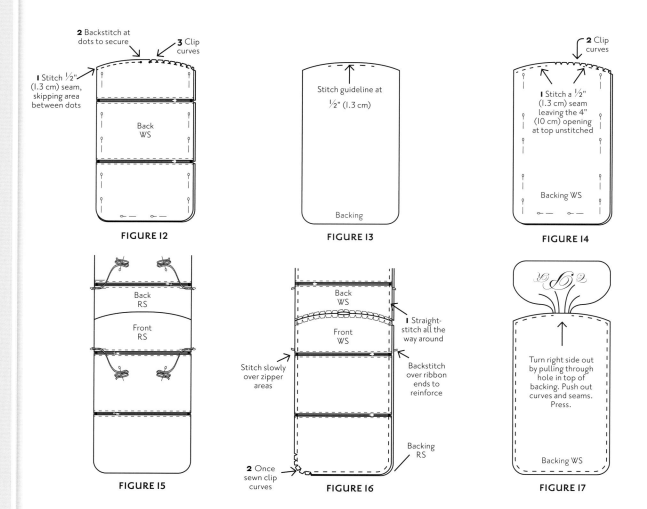

2 Backstitch at dots to secure   **3** Clip curves

1 Stitch ½" (1.3 cm) seam, skipping area between dots

Back WS

FIGURE 12

Stitch guideline at ½" (1.3 cm)

Backing

FIGURE 13

2 Clip curves

1 Stitch a ½" (1.3 cm) seam leaving the 4" (10 cm) opening at top unstitched

Backing WS

FIGURE 14

Back RS

Front RS

FIGURE 15

Back WS

Front WS

Stitch slowly over zipper areas

1 Straight-stitch all the way around

Backstitch over ribbon ends to reinforce

2 Once sewn clip curves

Backing RS

FIGURE 16

Turn right side out by pulling through hole in top of backing. Push out curves and seams. Press.

Backing WS

FIGURE 17

around the holder, stitching slowly over the zipper areas. Backstitch over the ribbon ends to ensure they are caught in the stitching. Trim the seam slightly to neaten. Clip the curves every ¼" (6 mm) **(FIG. 16)**.

6 Turn the holder through the opening in the lining **(FIG. 17)**. Push out the curves and seams flush with the stitched edge. Press.

7 Pin along the edges of the holder. Topstitch about ¼" (6 mm) from the edge, removing the pins as you stitch **(FIG. 18)**.

8 Glue-baste the lining to the holder opening in front and back. Be sure to align the opening for the hanger hook **(FIG. 19)**.

9 Topstitch ¼" (6 mm) on each side of the seam all the way across the curve **(FIG. 20)**.

10 Optional: Mark the vertical center of the top pocket on the holder front and topstitch using a triple straight stitch **(FIG. 21)**.

11 Cut four 6" (15 cm) pieces of silk satin ribbon. Fold each ribbon in half and slip the fold through the hole in the zipper slide. Insert the ribbon

tails through the ribbon loop and pull tightly **(FIGS. 22A–C)**. Hand-stitch the ribbon to prevent it from pulling out of the zipper slide.

12 The remaining ribbon may be wrapped around the hanger and tied into a bow to decorate the hanger hook.

13 Push the hanger hook through the opening in the top center of the holder, draping the holder over the hanger. Pull the bow through the opening in the holder so it is visible. Tie bows on each side of the holder to secure (see photo on page 118).

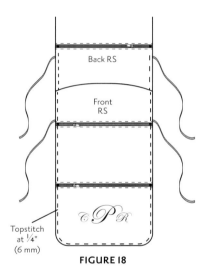

Topstitch at ¼" (6 mm)

FIGURE 18

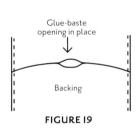

Glue-baste opening in place

Backing

FIGURE 19

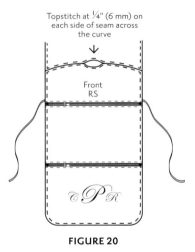

Topstitch at ¼" (6 mm) on each side of seam across the curve

Front RS

FIGURE 20

Front RS

Triple stitch at center

FIGURE 21

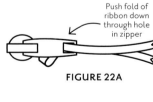

Push fold of ribbon down through hole in zipper

FIGURE 22A

Feed ribbon tails through loop

FIGURE 22B

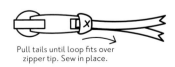

Pull tails until loop fits over zipper tip. Sew in place.

FIGURE 22C

Techniques

Neck Binding or Facing

(Assumes ⅝" [1.5 cm] seam allowance and will achieve a ¼" [6 mm] finished binding. Differing allowances will be listed in the instructions for individual patterns but the procedure is the same.)

1 Cut a piece of bias 2¼" (5.5 cm) wide and at least 1" (2.5 cm) longer than the measurement around the unfinished neckline edge. Fold the bias strip in half lengthwise (**FIG. 1**).

2 Press the bias strip into a circle following the curve of the neckline and with the fold on the outside of the circle. Pin the raw edge of the bias to the raw edge of the neckline right sides together with the end of the strip extending ½" (1.3 cm) off the garment edge. Fold back the ½" (1.3 cm) extensions and stitch to apply (**FIG. 2**).

3 Trim all the layers of the seam allowance to ¼" (6 mm). For a facing, clip the curved seams to the stitching line.

4 For a binding, wrap the bias band around the seam allowance and blindstitch to the stitching line of the seam (bias will show). For a facing, press the seam and the bias band to the inside of the garment and blindstitch along the folded edge catching only the lining, or making tiny stitches through the garment fabric (bias will not show).

NOTE: *For a bias finish with a collar, pin the collar to the neckline, fold back the shirt placket facings and baste* (**FIG. 4**), *then apply the bias; do not extend the ends of the bias beyond the garment edges* (**FIG. 5**).

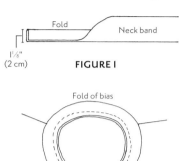

Fold · Neck band
1⅛" (2 cm)

FIGURE 1

Fold of bias · Right-side garments

FIGURE 2

Hand whip · Wrong-side garment

FIGURE 3

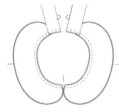

FIGURE 4

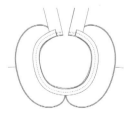

FIGURE 5

French Seam

1 Place the fabric pieces with wrong sides together. These instructions are based on a ½" (1.3 cm) seam allowance.

2 Zigzag (L=1.0; W=1.0) or lightening stitch (L=2.5; W=1.0) ¼" (6 mm) from the raw edge of the fabric (**FIG. 1**).

3 Trim the seam allowance close to the stitching (**SEE FIG. 1**).

4 Open out the fabric and press the seam to one side.

5 Fold the fabric along the seamline with the right sides together, encasing the zigzag stitching (**FIG. 2**).

6 Stitch a ¼" (6 mm) seam, enclosing the zigzag stitching (**FIG. 3**).

7 Press the seam to one side.

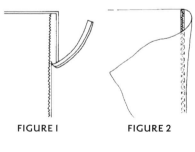

FIGURE 1 · **FIGURE 2**

FIGURE 3

Piping

1. Cut a bias strip 1¼" (3.2 cm) (or preferred width) wide by the length needed. The bias may be pieced so that the piping will be made in one long strip **(FIGS. 1 and 2)**.

2. Fold the bias strip in half lengthwise and finger press.

3. Place tiny cording along the center of the strip on the wrong side and fold the fabric over the cording, meeting the long edges of the fabric.

4. Use a zipper foot or pintuck foot (guiding the cord in a groove and moving the needle position) and stitch close to the cording but not through it **(FIG. 3)**.

5. Trim the seam allowance of the piping to equal the given seam allowance of your project **(FIG. 4)**.

Placket

1. Draw a 5" (12.5 cm) slit down the center of the back skirt from the top edge. Stitch just beside the line to the point and back up, leaving a ¹⁄₁₆" (2 mm) between. Cut down the line to the end of the stitching **(FIG. 1)**.

2. Press an 11" × 1½" (28 × 3.8 cm) placket strip in half lengthwise or use a ¾" (2 cm) wide strip cut from the selvage edge and do not fold). Pull the slit in the skirt apart to form a "V." Place the right side of the strip to the right side of the garment. The stitching will be made from the wrong side with the garment on top and the placket strip on the bottom. The placket strip will be straight and the garment will form a shallow "V" with the point of the "V" ¼" (6 mm) from the edge of the placket **(FIG. 2)**.

3. Stitch using a ¼" (6 mm) seam. It is important to catch a few fibers in the seam at the inner point of the "V" **(SEE FIG. 2)**.

4. Press the seam toward the fold/selvage edge of the placket strip. Turn the fold/selvage edge to the inside of the garment, enclosing the seam allowance. Stitch in place by hand or machine **(FIG. 3)**.

5. On the inside of the placket, stitch the placket at an angle from the lower inside edge of the folded edges **(FIG. 4)**.

6. The back of the garment will lap left over right. Fold the right side of the placket to the inside and pin. Leave the left back placket extended **(FIG. 5)**.

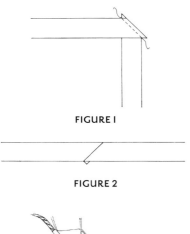

FIGURE 1

FIGURE 2

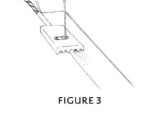

FIGURE 3

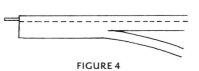

FIGURE 4

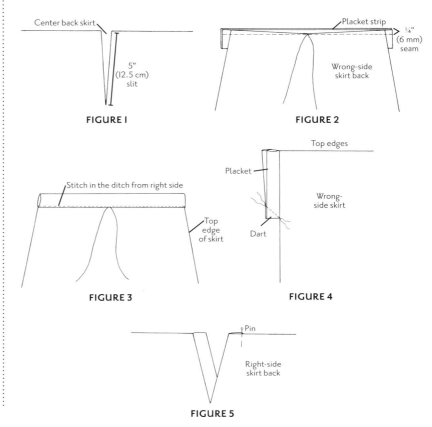

Center back skirt

5" (12.5 cm) slit

FIGURE 1

Placket strip

¼" (6 mm) seam

Wrong-side skirt back

FIGURE 2

Stitch in the ditch from right side

Top edge of skirt

FIGURE 3

Top edges

Placket

Wrong-side skirt

Dart

FIGURE 4

Pin

Right-side skirt back

FIGURE 5

Shark's Teeth

1 Begin with a rectangle of batiste the block size designated for your project; starch and press. Measure up from the bottom of the block 1⅝" (4 cm) and draw the first tuck line with a blue wash-away marking pen across the fabric, parallel to the bottom edge.

2 Place the fabric over the shark's teeth template (see Little Boy Blue on CD-rom) so that the drawn line on the fabric is directly on top of the bottom line of the template. Trace all the other foldlines, stitching lines and clip marks onto the fabric block **(FIG. 1)**.

3 Press a sharp crease exactly on each foldline. At each line, with the fabric folded, stitch a tuck by stitching with a straight stitch (L=2.0) exactly on the stitching line. Press the tucks down (so the clip marks are visible on top of the tucks) **(FIG. 2)**. Press again on the wrong side, making sure there are no extra folds of fabric at the stitching lines. The tucks should be fairly even, but not quite touching, with a gap of about ⅛" (3 mm) or less between the tucks.

4 On the right side, use a small, very sharp-pointed scissors to cut the clip marks on the bottom tuck only. Clip to, but not through the stitching line. HINT: *It's easiest to start at the bottom and work up and to work on only one row at a time. If you clip all the tucks at once, you have to fold all those little pieces out of the way as you stitch, and then they start to fray.*

5 Turn the piece wrong side up and fold up the bottom of the block so you are looking at the underside of the bottom clipped tuck. At each clip, fold the cut edges so they lie right along the stitching line, making a "V" at each clip **(FIG. 3)**. Press well and secure the folded corners with a tiny bit of water-soluble glue or glue stick. HINT: *Some "teeth" may have sharp, pointed tips, and some may have slightly squared-off tips. Don't worry about it. When the design is done, what you see is an overall pattern, not any individual "tooth."*

6 When all the clips on the bottom tuck have been folded, press from the right side to dry the glue. With the bottom of the block still folded out of the way—you will be stitching through the tuck only— zigzag (L=1.0; W=2.0) on the right side of the tuck so that one needle swing stitches right into the previous straight stitching and the other needle swing stitches into the tuck, catching the raw edges of the folded clips on the wrong side **(FIG. 4)**. At the "V's," one needle swing will stitch into the air only for a stitch or two.

7 Press this row of shark's teeth down. Repeat clipping, folding and stitching for the next row up. On this row, there will be a section in the center where the tuck is unclipped; continue zigzag stitching along this section of tuck. In other words, don't stop and start stitching where there are no clips.

8 Repeat for each tuck, moving up, doing all the steps for one tuck at a time.

9 Soak the fabric block in warm water to remove the markings and glue. Roll in a towel to remove excess water; then, press dry. Starch lightly and press dry again.

NOTE: *Drawings reflect hem of Little Boy Blue gown.*

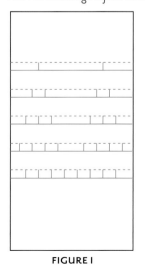

FIGURE 1

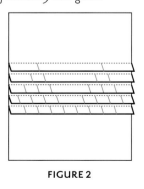

FIGURE 2

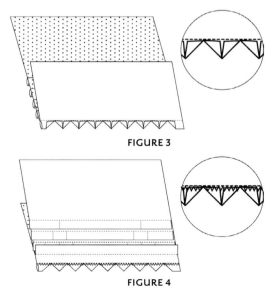

FIGURE 3

FIGURE 4

Appliqué
General Machine Appliqué Directions

1 Never start stitching at a corner or point; start at a straight side or curve (**FIG. 1**).

2 Position the appliqué piece so that the left swing of the needle (zig) stitches on the appliqué piece and the right swing of the needle (zag) stitches off the appliqué piece.

3 To tie on, take several straight stitches on the base fabric just off the appliqué edge. This stitching will be covered by the appliqué stitch (**FIG. 2**).

4 Set the machine to the desired zigzag width and length. If a "needle down" option is available on your machine, engage it; it will be helpful in satin stitching and pivoting. Reposition the project under the needle so that the zigzag stitches are placed mostly on the appliqué but extend completely off the edge of the appliqué. This will stitch the appliqué piece on in a neat fashion encasing the raw edges of the appliqué. If the entire stitch is taken on the appliqué, fuzzies may occur on the edge of the appliqué piece. If you don't stitch enough of the appliqué fabric, the appliqué may pull away from the stitching.

5 Take all stitches perpendicular to the edge of the appliqué (**FIG. 3**).

6 Stitch individual pieces and detail lines working background to foreground.

7 Do not push or pull but simply guide the fabric through the machine. Let the machine do the work. A gentle nudge may be required when crossing over previous stitching.

8 To tie off, change to a short straight stitch and reposition the project under the presser foot so that the needle is just beside the end of the satin stitching; take several tiny straight stitches just beside the satin stitching.

9 Cut threads very close to the stitching.

10 With a water-soluble marker, transfer any straight-stitch detail not previously satin-stitched. These can be stitched in free-motion embroidery, hand embroidery, programmed machine stitches, or digitized machine embroidery.

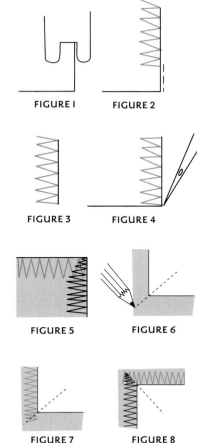

FIGURE 1   FIGURE 2

FIGURE 3   FIGURE 4

FIGURE 5   FIGURE 6

FIGURE 7   FIGURE 8

Outside Corner

1 Place the left swing of the needle on the appliqué piece.

2 Zigzag along the appliqué as described in Steps 1–7 of General Machine Appliqué Directions.

3 Stitch down the first side to the corner, stopping with the needle down at the point of the corner (**FIG. 4**).

4 Pivot 90 degrees. Lower the foot. Note the stitch width used.

5 Raise the needle from the fabric, change to right needle position and a 0 stitching width. Reposition so that the needle pierces the same hole of the last stitch before the pivot. Guide the fabric with the left hand while gradually increasing the stitch width with the right hand, stopping at the original width setting (**FIG. 5**). Watch where your needle is stitching, not the stitch width knob or button.

Inside Corner

1 Place the left swing of the needle on the appliqué piece.

2 Mark line bisecting the inside corner with water-soluble marker (**FIG. 6**).

3 Zigzag along the appliqué as described in Steps 1–7 of General Machine Appliqué Directions.

4 Stitch down the first side until the left swing of the needle intersects the drawn line (**FIG. 7**).

5 Leaving the needle down, raise the foot, pivot 90 degrees, and lower the foot. Note the stitch width being used.

6 Raise the needle from the fabric. Change to the left needle position and a 0 stitch width. Reposition so that the needle pierces the same hole of the last stitch before the pivot.

7 Guide the fabric with the left hand while gradually increasing the stitch width with the right hand, stopping at the original width setting (**FIG. 8**). It will be helpful to watch where your needle is stitching, not the stitch width knob or button.

French Sewing
Gathered Fabric to Entredeux

1 Run two rows of basting stitches to gather the fabric.

2 Pin the entredeux to the edge of the gathering.

3 Stitch in the ditch of the entredeux, and then stitch a second row ¹⁄₁₆" (1.5 mm) away from the first row of stitching. Trim the seam.

4 Roll and whip the seam with a tight zigzag, setting machine tension on 2 or 3. Suggested width=3; length=.75.

5 Press the entredeux away from the fabric and seam down.

6 From the right side, zigzag once again along the edge of the join. This will hold the seam down on the back side. Suggested width=1/5; length=2.

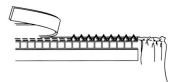

Lace Edging to Fabric

1 Align the edge of the lace ¹⁄₈" (3 mm) from the raw edge of the fabric and roll and whip together with a tight zigzag, setting the machine tension to 2 or 3. Suggested width=3.5; length=.5.

2 The fabric edge rolls into the stitching.

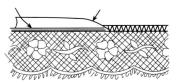

Lace to Entredeux

1 Trim one edge from the entredeux.

2 Butt the edge of the lace to the trimmed side of the entredeux and zigzag. Suggested width=2.5–3.5; length 2.5.

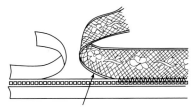

Lace to Lace

1 Butt the laces together under the presser foot starting about ½" (1.3 cm) from the end.

2 Zigzag stitch over the lace headings to join them. Suggested width=2–3; length=1 to 1.5.

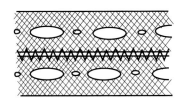

Gathered Lace to Entredeux

1 Pull the header thread in the lace edging to gather it.

2 Butt the gathered edge of the lace to the trimmed edge of the entredeux and zigzag in the same manner as the flat lace to entredeux. Suggested width=.5; length=2.

Entredeux to Fabric

1 Place the entredeux and fabric right sides together, aligning the edges.

2 Stitch in the ditch of the entredeux.

3 Stitch a second row ¹⁄₁₆" (2 mm) from the first row. Trim the seam very close to the second row of stitching.

4 Press the entredeux up.

5 Roll and whip with a zigzag; tension set on 2 or 3. Suggested width= 2.5 –3; length=1.

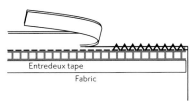

Entredeux tape
Fabric

Entredeux to Gathered Fabric

1 Trim the seam allowance of the entredeux to measure ¼" (6 mm).

2 Gather the fabric edge with two gathering rows at ¹⁄₈" (3 mm) and ³⁄₈" (1 cm).

3 Place the gathered fabric to the entredeux, right sides together. Stitch in the ditch with a regular straight stitch.

4 Stitch again, ¹⁄₁₆" (2 mm) away from the first stitching.

5 Trim the seam allowance to ¹⁄₈" (3 mm). Zigzag over the seam allowance. Suggested width=1.5; length=2.5.

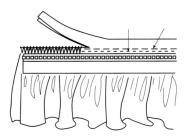

Lace Shaping

1 Place the project on a lace-shaping board with right side facing up. Place the pins at an angle through the lace heading into the board along the outer curve of the loop. Allow the beginning of the lace to extend past the end of the loop about ¼" (6 mm) (**FIG. 1**).

2 At the miter, place one pin at A and one at B (**FIG. 2**).

3 Fold the lace back on itself snugly at A and re-pin through both layers of lace at B (**FIG. 3**).

4 Continue shaping the other side of the lace loop, allowing the lace to extend past the end of the loop. Cut the lace about ¼" (6 mm) past the end of the loop (**FIG. 4**).

5 Pull the uppermost thread in the lace heading along the inside of the loop so the lace lies flat against the fabric (**FIG. 5**).

6 Turn the extended lace ends under even with the template line (**FIG. 6**).

7 Lightly starch, cover with a press cloth, and press each lace-shaped loop.

8 Re-pin the lace through the lace and fabric only. Remove the fabric from the board.

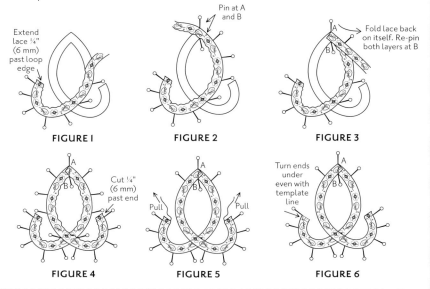

FIGURE I   FIGURE 2   FIGURE 3

FIGURE 4   FIGURE 5   FIGURE 6

Buttonhole Edge Scallop

1 Outline the scallops with a long running stitch, keeping as much thread on top of the fabric as possible (**FIG. 1**).

2 When approaching the tops, sew under two threads and stitch across the points holding the needle horizontally (**FIG. 2**).

3 Tie on with a new thread by stitching a running stitch inside the outlined boundary of the first scallop. Bring the needle out at the lower edge of the scallop, holding the thread down (**FIG. 3**).

4 Stitch from the upper edge of the running stitch to the lower edge of the running stitch with the thread behind the needle, picking up on the fabric that lies within the boundaries. Tighten. To work the next stitch, place it just beside the first, readjusting the angle of the needle as needed (**FIG. 4**).

5 Stitch the entire scallop, tapering the length as the outline dictates. When approaching the tips, place as many stitches as will comfortably fit, then switch to the next scallop, leaving the tip unstitched (**FIG. 5**).

6 Once all the scalloping is complete, trim away the fabric from beneath, being careful not to cut through the purls. To tie off, sew down over the last purl, and then slide the needle through the stitches on the back. It's always best to end and begin a new thread at the points (**FIG. 6**).

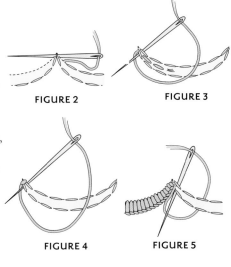

FIGURE 2   FIGURE 3

FIGURE 4   FIGURE 5

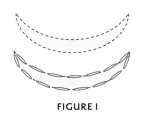

FIGURE I

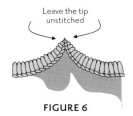

FIGURE 6

Attaching Tatting

1 Remove the chain-stitched header from the tatted edging to expose the picots.

2 Hand-stitch each picot loop to the fold edge of a finished edge or hem by sewing into the fabric and exiting at the picot loop, sewing through the loop and then back into the fabric edge at the same time.

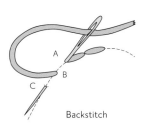

Attaching tatting

Backstitch

1 To begin, tie on with a split backstitch on the design line.

2 Take a short stitch from A to B and out at C, a stitch length away from B, covering the tie-on stitch. Each stitch should be placed head to toe, each sharing a hole with the previous stitch.

Backstitch

Eyelet

1 Sew a running stitch around the circle, taking tiny nips in the fabric (**FIG. 1**).

2 Open the center with a stiletto making sure to open it entirely. The side of the stiletto should brush up against the running stitches (**FIG. 2**).

3 Work a series of closely laid whipstitches around the edge of the opening, sewing into the hole and out on the outside edge of the running stitch. Feel free to reopen the center as many times as necessary (**FIG 3**).

4 To tie off, sew very close to the stitches, but not through the same hole as the last stitch to bring the needle to the back of the work. Make the stitch as short as possible and as close to the stitches as possible (**FIG. 4**).

5 Sew through a few stitches on back to tie off (**FIG. 5**).

6 Re-shape the eyelet once it is completed (**FIG. 6**).

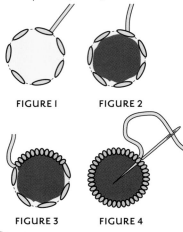

FIGURE 1   FIGURE 2

FIGURE 3   FIGURE 4

Wrong side

FIGURE 5   FIGURE 6

Teardrop Cut Eyelet

1 Outline the shape as usual with a running stitch, beginning at the edge where the rounded portion starts to straighten, placing the stitches directly on the design line and ending at the starting place (**FIG. 1**).

2 Inside the round end of the eyelet, open the area with a stiletto until it is sufficiently opened. Work the rounded edge of the teardrop as a traditional eyelet. Stop stitching where the rounded edge begins, and then park the needle leaving the thread attached (**FIG. 2**).

3 With very sharp scissors, carefully snip from the opening to the tip down the center with pointed scissors, vertically (**FIG. 3**).

4 Turn the raw edge points of fabric under the back with the needle, and taking small whipstitches over the fold and the running stitch, work around the shape (**FIG. 4**). When stitching the point, make a longer stitch to accentuate the shape. Taper the two stitches on both sides slightly.

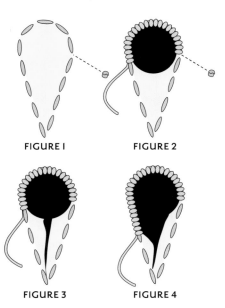

FIGURE 1   FIGURE 2

FIGURE 3   FIGURE 4

5 Complete the remaining edge of the eyelet as before, and then join the stitches together seamlessly on the edge (**FIG. 5**). Bring the needle to the back of the work, sewing very close to the embroidered edge through the fabric.

6 Tie off on back by sliding the needle through the stitches. The points of the fabric on the back of the work are cut away (**FIG. 6**).

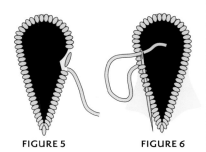

FIGURE 5   FIGURE 6

Bullion Rosebud

1 Using one strand of floss and a round-eyed needle, begin with an upward split-backstitch on the right side of the fabric, in the center of the design area. Sew out at A, and then into the fabric at point B and out at point A. Do not pull the thread through. Push the needle through until only the eye remains (**FIG. 1**).

2 Wrap the thread around the needle clockwise. Be especially careful to pull tautly on the first wrap, making sure that the thread is close against the fabric. Continue wrapping the needle until the depth of the wraps is equal to the length of the "bite" in the fabric, minus one wrap (**FIG. 2**).

3 Pin the wraps between your thumb and forefinger, and then gently pull the needle through while holding the wraps securely and realigning the knot in the space between

A and B. Continue to pull the tension out until all the slack is almost completely removed from the thread, and then let up on the tension slightly and continue to tighten allowing the wraps to taper slightly (**FIG. 3**).

4 Sew in at B, and then out at A to begin the next bullion, taking every advantage to re-tighten the wraps as necessary (**FIG. 4**).

5 Insert the needle in at B and out at A, but do not pull the needle through. Wrap the needle as before with one additional wrap than the first knot. Gently pull the needle through the wraps (**FIG. 5**).

6 Tighten the bullion as before, curving the knot as you tighten, slightly inward to form the bud. End the stitch by sewing in at B and tying off on the back by sewing through the mound a few times (**FIG. 6**).

7 Begin with a bullion bud stitched in the desired color floss to form the bud of the rose. Tie-on with green and the same needle by weaving the thread tail through the stitches on the back. Position the bud horizontally. Sew out at A (**FIG. 7**).

8 Re-insert the needle in at B and out at A, leaving the tip of the needle exposed. Do not pull it through. Wrap the thread ten to thirteen times around the needle clockwise. Be especially careful to pull tautly on the first wrap, making sure that the thread is right against the bud (**FIG. 8**).

9 Pinch the wraps between your thumb and forefinger, and then gently pull the needle through while holding the wraps securely. Continue to pull the thread through the wraps until the slack is almost completely removed from

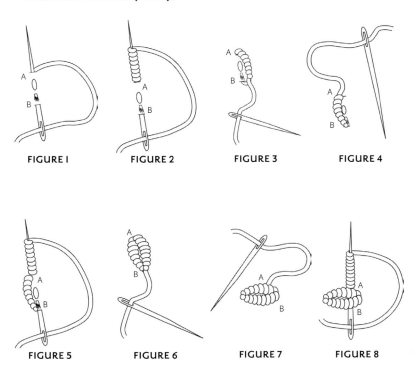

FIGURE 1   FIGURE 2   FIGURE 3   FIGURE 4

FIGURE 5   FIGURE 6   FIGURE 7   FIGURE 8

the thread, and then swing the thread tail around the broad base of the bud, tightening and curving the bullion around the bud (**FIG. 9**).

10 Take the needle down at B bringing the thread to the back of the work. Tighten the stitch completely (**FIG. 10**).

11 Stitch the leaves as lazy daisy stitch and then tie off on the back by sliding the needle through the stitches on the back (**FIG. 11**).

12 To make a large bud, begin with a standard rosebud, but do not taper the top as much, yielding a squattier-shaped bud. Add a wrap around the remaining edge of the flower with green.

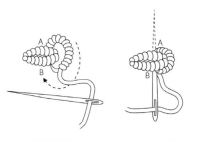

FIGURE 9   FIGURE 10

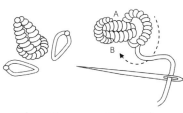

FIGURE 11   FIGURE 12

Full Bullion Rose

1 Follow Steps 1–6 of the Bullion Rosebud, but do not tie off after the second knot. To make the third knot, insert the needle in B and out A, but do not pull the needle through. Wrap the exposed tip of the needle the same number of wraps as before (**FIG. 1**).

2 Pull the thread through while holding the wraps, and then tighten the loop as much as possible until the knot lies flat against the fabric. Insert the needle down at B to end the three-knot bullion. Tie off on the back (**FIG. 2**).

3 Tie on at the back of the mound and then emerge at C. Sew in at D and out at C but do not pull the needle through. Wrap the needle a total of eleven to thirteen wraps (**FIG. 3**).

4 Pin the wraps between your forefinger and thumb as before, and then slide the needle through while holding the wraps. Tighten around the edge of the center

flower, and then sew down at D to complete the swirl (**FIG. 4**).

5 Rotate the work 180 degrees and emerge at E, the top edge of the center bullion just beside the previous stitch (**FIG. 5**).

6 Sew in at F and out at E, but don't pull the needle through. Wrap the tip of the needle a total of eleven to thirteen wraps. Pin the wraps between your forefinger and thumb while holding the wraps, and then pull the needle through (**FIG. 6**).

7 Tighten the wraps completely, and then insert the needle in at F to complete the stitch (**FIG. 7**). Rotate the flower 90 degrees to work the next petals.

8 To form the side petals, bring the needle out at G (the upper edge of the flower), and then sew in at H and out at G, but do not pull the needle through. Wrap the tip of the needle the same number of wraps as before, about eleven to thirteen times (**FIG. 8**).

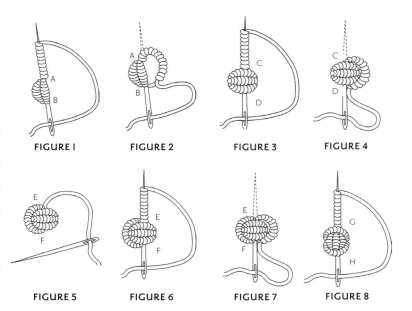

FIGURE 1   FIGURE 2   FIGURE 3   FIGURE 4

FIGURE 5   FIGURE 6   FIGURE 7   FIGURE 8

9 Pinch the wraps, pull the needle through and tighten the stitch. To end the stitch, sew down at H and tighten the stitch (**FIG. 9**).

10 Rotate the bullion 180 degrees. Sew out at |, and then sew in at K and out at |, but do not pull the needle through. Wrap the tip of the needle the same number of wraps as before (**FIG. 10**).

11 Pinch the wraps between your forefinger and thumb, and then slide the needle through while holding the wraps in place. Swing the bullion toward the flower, curving the petal around the edge of the bullion center as you tighten the stitch. Bring the needle down at K to complete the flower (**FIG. 11**).

12 Tie off on the back by sewing through the mound a few times. This bullion rose is completed, but for a more elaborate flower, add bullion loops around the flower center, if desired.

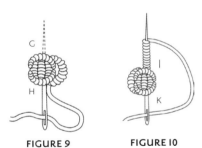

FIGURE 9   FIGURE 10

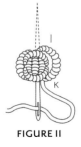

FIGURE 11

Large Full Bullion

1 Complete a full bullion flower, and then tie off on the back. On the wrong side, tie on with white floss. Bring the needle out at A (to the left of the center), sew in at B and out again at A but do not pull the needle through. Wrap the needle eleven to thirteen times, clockwise (**FIG. 1**).

2 Pinch the wraps between your forefinger and thumb, and then slide the needle through while holding the wraps. Curve the bullion knot around the edge of the center flower. Tighten the stitch, and then insert the needle in at B to complete the stitch (**FIG. 2**).

3 Emerge at C, a third of the way back. Sew from D to C, the same distance away, leaving the tip of the needle exposed. Do not pull the needle clockwise the same number of wraps as the previous knot. Pull the needle through the wraps and tighten (**FIG. 3**).

4 Tighten while curving the bullion around the outside edge of the center flower, insert the needle into D, and bring the thread to the back. The following bullions will all be the same length but each will overlap the previous bullion by one third of the length (**FIG. 4**).

5 Bring the needle out at E, slightly to the right of the center and about a third of the way back, and then sew from F to E leaving the tip of the needle exposed. Wrap the tip of the needle as before, the same number of wraps (**FIG. 5**).

6 Hold the wraps between your fingers and thumb, and then pull the wraps through. Tighten as before while curving the knot around the outer edge of the center flower. Sew down at F (**FIG. 6**).

7 Sew out at G, and then sew from H to G, but do not pull the needle through. Wrap the tip of the needle the same number of times as before (**FIG. 7**).

8 Pull the wraps through as before, and then tighten while swirling around the center flower. Sew into H to bring the thread tail to the back (**FIG. 8**).

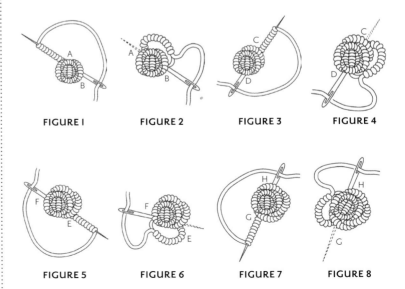

FIGURE 1   FIGURE 2   FIGURE 3   FIGURE 4

FIGURE 5   FIGURE 6   FIGURE 7   FIGURE 8

9 Sew out at |, and then sew from K to | leaving the tip of the needle exposed. Wrap the tip the same number of times as before (**FIG. 9**).

10 Pull the wraps through as before, and then tighten while swirling round the center flower. Sew into K to bring the thread tail to the back (**FIG. 10**).

11 The completed flower (**FIG. 11**). You may or may not need to add a fifth petal to complete your flower.

12 To tie off, bring the thread to the wrong side of the work. Sew through the stitches on the back without going through the fabric, and then switch direction and repeat (**FIG. 12**).

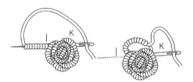

FIGURE 9 **FIGURE 10**

Wrong side

FIGURE 11 **FIGURE 12**

Granito

(Granito usually contains up to twelve stitches, all stitched in the same A-B point).

1 With one strand of floss and a #10 crewel needle, sew a stitch inside the "white space" of the circle to tie on with a split-backstitch (**FIG. 1**).

2 Leaving the tail of the thread very close to its end, sew back into the center of the circle, splitting through the thread in the process and exiting on the edge of the circle. Tighten the stitch well (**FIG. 2**).

3 To work the first stitch, sew from one edge of the circle to the other (A to B). Pull the stitch tightly. If the fabric puckers, the tension is correct. Trim thread tail, if necessary (**FIG. 3**).

4 Holding the thread up and away, work the next four stitches in the same A-B points, pulling each stitch tightly. Don't pay too much attention to where the threads are placed, but be sure to enter the same two points each time. Work a total of five stitches (**FIG. 4**).

5 Work the next two stitches in the same A-B points as before, allowing them to fall off the mound and lie to the left, widening the shape and forming more of a ball-like shape (**FIG. 5**).

6 Work the next two stitches in the same A-B points as before, allowing them to fall off the mound and lie to the right to widen the shape to the right (**FIG. 6**).

7 With the remaining stitches, stitch into the same A-B points and allow the threads to fall over the top of the mound to smooth any rough areas. Use as many as you feel necessary (**FIG. 7**).

8 Bring the needle to the wrong side of the fabric, and then tie off by sewing through the mound on the back a few times (**FIG. 8**).

9 When working a granitos flower, make the center granito first, and then form the petals around the center, aligning the A-B points radiating from the center of the flower. Do not trail threads between granitos (**FIG. 9**).

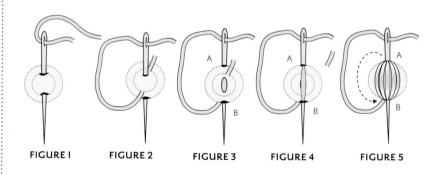

FIGURE 1 **FIGURE 2** **FIGURE 3** **FIGURE 4** **FIGURE 5**

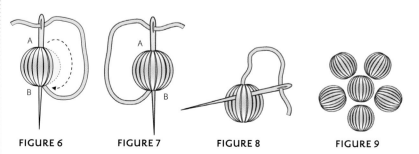

FIGURE 6 **FIGURE 7** **FIGURE 8** **FIGURE 9**

Lazy Daisy

1 With one strand of green floss, tie on inside the narrow end of the leaf close to the center with one split-backstitch. Bring the needle out at the base of the leaf at A (**FIG. 1**).

2 While holding the thread loop down, sew in at A and out at B on the outer edge of the leaf, holding the thread loop beneath the needle (**FIG. 2**).

3 Tighten the stitch keeping the tension slight, but pulling it sufficiently until the loop lies flat. To complete the stitch, place a tacking stitch over the thread loop at C, just long enough to match the thickness of the thread (**FIG. 3**).

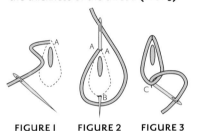

| FIGURE 1 | FIGURE 2 | FIGURE 3 |

Lazy Daisy Flower

(best worked in a hoop with fabric as tight as possible)

1 With a blue wash-away marking pen, divide the circle into four equal

sections, as shown. Tie on inside the broad end of the circle close to the center with two backstitches. Bring the needle out at the innermost cross section of the circle at A (**FIG. 1**).

2 While holding the thread loop down, sew in at A and out at B on the outer edge of the circle, holding the thread beneath the needle (**FIG. 2**).

3 Tighten the stitch, keeping the tension slight, but pulling it sufficiently until the loop lies flat. To complete the stitch, place a tacking stitch over the thread loop at C, just long enough to match the thickness of the thread (**FIG. 3**).

4 Rotate the work, and then bring the needle out at the new A position, in order to work the next petal along the cross section (**FIG. 4**).

5 Complete the first four "pilot" petals at each cross section of the circle. Emerge along the inner circle to fill in the open spaces with clusters of petals within the four pilot petals (**FIG. 5**).

6 Fill each open space with as many petals as will fit comfortably, completing one space at a time. Notice the inner stitches are placed closer than the outer stitches (**FIG. 6**).

7 Bring the needle out in the center of the flower to begin the French knots (**FIG. 7**).

8 To begin French knot, straighten the thread tail, holding it about 4" (10 cm) away from point A. Position the needle over the thread tail, forming a cross while holding the thread straight (**FIG. 8**).

9 With your non-stitching hand, wrap the thread loop around the tip of the needle, counterclockwise one time (**FIG. 9**).

10 Insert the tip of the needle into the fabric just slightly above the entry point. Tighten the loop very close to the fabric while holding the needle (**FIG. 10**).

11 Pop the needle through the wrap and sew through until the stitch is tightened. If the knot is dimpled, the stitch was correctly made. If larger knots are desired, add strands, not wraps (**FIG. 11**).

12 To work the next knot, bring the needle up very close to the previous knot and repeat Steps 8–11. Fill in the center of the flower with as many knots as necessary (**FIG. 12**). Tie off on the back, weaving the thread through the stitches.

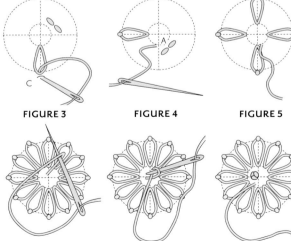

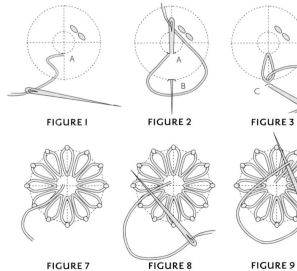

| FIGURE 1 | FIGURE 2 | FIGURE 3 | FIGURE 4 | FIGURE 5 | FIGURE 6 |

| FIGURE 7 | FIGURE 8 | FIGURE 9 | FIGURE 10 | FIGURE 11 | FIGURE 12 |

Padded Satin Stitch

1 Tie on inside the leaf shape with two backstitches. Place them in any direction. Beginning at the tip, stitch a long backstitch, bringing the stitch out past the point slightly. Work a split-stitch around the outer edge of the leaf (**FIG. 1**).

2 Line pad the inside with one to four straight stitches in reversing directions to keep as little thread on back as possible. Stitch the center stitch first, A to B (**FIG. 2**).

3 Emerge just outside the foundation stitches at the widest point, and then stitch over the width of the leaf to the other edge of the foundation stitches from A to B (**FIG. 3**).

4 Work the next and all concurrent stitches the same way, placing them side-by-side. When the shape starts to diminish, begin curving the stitches by stitching very close to the previous entry points (**FIG. 4**).

5 Complete the first section of the leaf, and then bring the needle out at the start of the remaining section (**FIG. 5**).

6 Complete the leaf shape, placing the stitches one beside the other, angling the needle in the direction of the previous stitch, not toward the foundation stitches (**FIG. 6**). Tie off on the back by sliding the threads through the stitches on back.

FIGURE 1

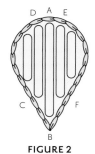

FIGURE 2

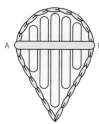

FIGURE 3

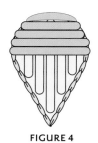

FIGURE 4

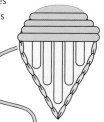

FIGURE 5

FIGURE 6

Shadow Stitched Leaf

1 Tie on at the tip of the leaf with a split-backstitch in position of the first stitch. Work the shape upward, beginning in the "V" configuration, and then proceed to stitch the backstitches alternating sides and using the center vein as a stitching boundary (**FIG. 1**).

2 When approaching the top edge of the shape, you will run out of stitching area on the vein. Keep on stitching from side to side, using the boundary on the edge of the leaf as an alternate boundary. Fill in the shape with backstitches to fill, once the line begins to straighten (**FIG. 2**).

3 To stitch the opposite edge of the leaf, use the center vein to piggyback the stitches, placing them in the same A-B points as before. Tie off on the back by sliding the thread beneath the stitches on the back (**FIG. 3**).

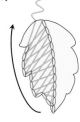

FIGURE 1

FIGURE 2

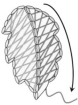

FIGURE 3

Split Stitch

(used as a sturdy foundation for a padded satin stitch)

1 Enter the fabric on the design line. Stitch a slightly long stitch A to B (**FIG. 1**).

2 Begin the next stitch by stitching up through the existing stitch, splitting it in the process. Stitch a stitch the same length as before (**FIG. 2**).

3 Continue stitching in this manner, having all consecutive stitches, always beginning inside the previous stitch (**FIG. 3**).

4 To end the stitch, sew forward a stitch length away and bring the thread to the wrong side (**FIG. 4**). Weave the thread through the stitches on back.

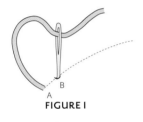

FIGURE 1

FIGURE 2

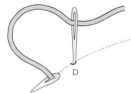

FIGURE 3

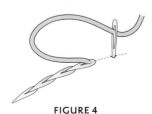

FIGURE 4

Spoke Flower

1 Insert a straight pin vertically through the inner circle of the design. Insert a straight pin horizontally through the inner circle. Tie on inside the circle with two tiny backstitches. Emerge close to the inner circle at the first pin (**FIG. 1**).

2 Wrap the thread tail around the circle, slipping the thread beneath the pin each time. Upon reaching the starting point after the first rotation, pull the stitches tight against the base of the pins (**FIG. 2**).

3 Continue coiling the thread around the center of the spoke, filling in the space entirely while keeping the threads even and one beside the other (**FIG. 3**).

4 When reaching the starting point, and when there are enough rows to cover the circle space, stop coiling (**FIG. 4**).

5 Bring the needle down to the back of the work at the starting point on the outer edge of the spiral (**FIG. 5**).

6 Sew out at the center circle just beside the straight pin (**FIG. 6**).

7 Tack the stitch down on the outer edge of the circle, keeping the stitch straight. Emerge at the next pin position close to inner circle and pin (**FIG. 7**).

8 Go back to the center of the flower at each pin position, and then tack the straight stitch over the wraps and into the fabric beside the pins (**FIG. 8**).

9 To finish the spoke flower, tie off in the center of the shape with two tiny backstitches (**FIG. 9**).

10 Tie on with a yellow thread and work a small group of French knots in the center of the flower. Tie off on the back by sliding the needle through the stitches (**FIG. 10**).

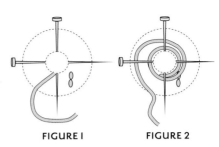

FIGURE 1   FIGURE 2

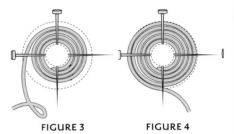

FIGURE 3   FIGURE 4

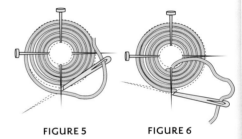

FIGURE 5   FIGURE 6

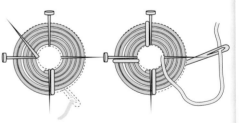

FIGURE 7   FIGURE 8

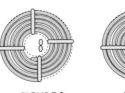

FIGURE 9   FIGURE 10

Smocking Stitch

Cable

1 Come up in the pleat valley on a gathering row, carry the floss over two pleats to the right, stitch into the right side of the second pleat and out the opposite side, keeping the needle horizontal and the floss below the needle (**FIG. 1**). This creates a down cable (**FIG. 2**).

2 With the floss above the needle, stitch through the next pleat to the left from the right side of the pleat, and out the left side, again keeping the needle horizontal (**FIG. 3**). This creates an up cable (**FIG. 4**).

3 To create a cable row, continue in this same fashion keeping the floss above and below the needle for every other stitch.

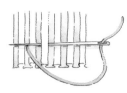

FIGURE I

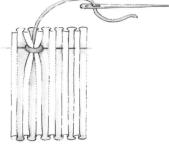

FIGURE 2

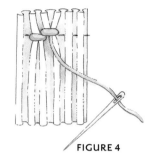

FIGURE 3

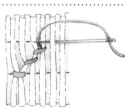

FIGURE 4

Trellis

1 Working between two gather rows, bring the needle to the front on the left-hand side of the first pleat on the bottom gathering row. With the thread below the needle, stitch a down cable (**FIG. 1**).

2 Move up halfway between the two gathering rows for the next stitch. With the needle parallel to the gathering thread and the thread below the needle, take a stitch in the next pleat (**FIG. 2**). This will create the first step up (**SEE FIG. 1**).

3 Move up to the top gather row. With the needle parallel to the gathering thread and the thread below the needle, take a stitch in the next pleat. (**SEE FIG. 2**). This will create the second step up.

4 With the thread above the needle, stitch a top cable on the top gathering row (this is the turn-around stitch) (**SEE FIG. 2**).

5 Move down halfway between the two gathering rows for the next stitch. With the needle parallel to

the gathering thread and the thread above the needle, take a stitch in the next pleat. This will create the first step down (**FIG. 3**).

6 Move down to the bottom gathering row. With the needle parallel to the gathering thread and the thread above the needle, take a stitch in the next pleat. This will create the second step down (**FIG. 4**).

7 With the thread below the needle, stitch a down cable on the bottom gathering row (this is the turn-around stitch) (**FIG. 5**).

8 Repeat Steps 2–7 to continue the pattern across the pleats. For a diamond pattern, repeat instructions between top gathering row and next one above in a mirror image. At each valley, upper and lower cables will sit on top of each other.

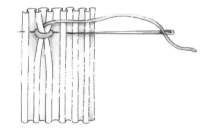

FIGURE 2

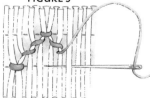

FIGURE 3

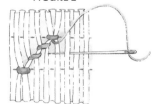

FIGURE 4

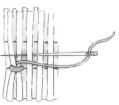

FIGURE I

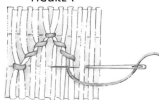

FIGURE 5

Closed Herringbone Stitch

Shadow embroidery (closed herringbone), simply put, is basically a backstitch. But the backstitch is taken alternately from one boundary point to another. The stitches are lined up head to toe and share holes. Usually the stitches are very short, less than 1/16" (2 mm) long, and it is important that they be stitched carefully so as not to "jump the track" of the stitching line. The stitches look pretty when they are placed exactly on the drawn line so take extra care to trace your design exactly.

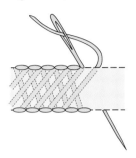

Piggybacking

This term applies to the technique of stitching over an existing stitch. This is only done when two shapes share a common wall. The stitch is taken into the exact two A-B points as the previous section. If the two shapes are the same color, the stitches lie on top of each other. If they are different, they lie side-by-side, but are still sharing the same holes.

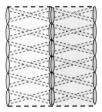

Shadow Embroidery Odd Shapes

Diamond

This shape is the easiest of all to stitch. Begin at the "V" and work the shape in the V-configuration. Start with a backstitch away from the point. Both backstitches join together at the point and share a hole. End in the V-configuration to complete the section.

Triangle

This shape is stitched just like the diamond shape, but when reaching the top portion of the shape, stitch a row of regular backstitches across to enclose the area. The stitching does not continue to alternate from edge to edge when the line is straight.

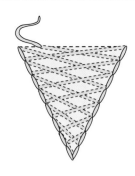

Rectangle

On the shortest stretch of space (across the bottom), stitch a row of regular backstitches. When your last stitch reaches the end of the wall, begin the side-to-side progression. When the sides are stitched, just fill in the top portion with a row of regular backstitches to enclose the area.

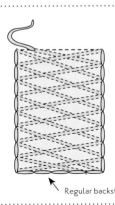

Regular backstitches

Oval

Since this shape does not have a recognizable starting point, begin by stitching a few regular backstitches on one edge. Once the wall of the area begins to arch upward, begin the side-to-side progression. Complete the shape with backstitches once the line straightens out.

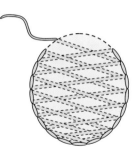

Heart

This shape represents "encroached" shapes; those that begin as one and split into two or more shapes. Begin at the "V" and work the stitches upward. Once the inward peak begins to encroach on the crossover stitches, complete each arch separately.

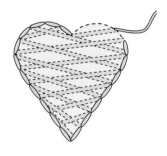

Star

The shape represents an irregular shape with various starting points. Look for the horizontal line, and then start at the most obvious point. Work the stitches from left to right, up to the nearest wall, then use the horizontal line to travel to the farthest wall. Begin crossover stitches, and then work the shape as you would an encroached shape.

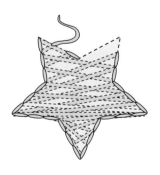

Clover

Begin by stitching the center of the flower in granito stitch. Working from the point of the first petal, begin stitching from side to side as you would a heart shape. When approaching the inward point, the shape divides into two shapes (**FIG. 1**).

Complete the first arch of the heart, and then bring the needle out at the inside edge of the remaining arch in the position of the first stitch (**FIG. 2**).

Complete the remaining section of the first petal, and then move the next shape without tying off (**FIG. 3**).

Complete the petal the same as the first, and then move to the next petal in line. When stitching adjoining walls, the stitches are "piggybacked" by stitching into the same exact A-B points as the existing stitches (**FIG. 4**).

Complete the design by stitching one French knot in the center of each petal close to the center granito. Tie off on the back through the granito (**FIG. 5**).

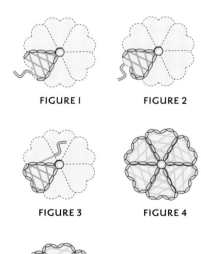

FIGURE 1   **FIGURE 2**

FIGURE 3   **FIGURE 4**

FIGURE 5

Tulip

Begin by stitching the leaf, beginning at the tip and working upward to the opposite tip. Work the stem in back-stitch (**FIG. 1**).

To work the tulip, begin at the base of the flower and work upward. When the crossover stitch reaches the inward point, complete the first section of the flower's top edge (**FIG. 2**).

Without tying off, proceed to the next tip of the flower and work as it as before (**FIG. 3**).

The completed tulip: The dot is worked in granito stitch and can be completed prior to stitching the tulip or after (**FIG. 4**).

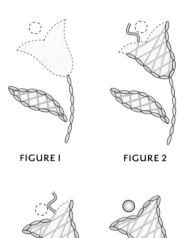

FIGURE 1   **FIGURE 2**

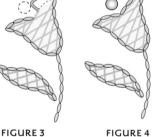

FIGURE 3   **FIGURE 4**

Contributors

LAURIE ANDERSON is from Columbia, Tennessee, and owns Southern Stitches Fine Heirloom Sewing and Custom-made Embroideries (*www.southern-stitches.com*). She is also owner of Brer Rabbit Designs (*www.brerrabitdesigns.com*), a website devoted to her classic children's wear sewing patterns and unique machine-embroidery designs. She is a commissioned designer with *Sew Beautiful* magazine. Her love for heirloom sewing and smocking began after the birth of her children, who are now grown. She now enjoys designing and sewing for her grandchildren, as well as for *Sew Beautiful*.

KATHY BARNARD served as senior editor for *Sew Beautiful* magazine for 19 years. Prior to joining Martha Pullen Company in 1992 as an illustrator, Kathy was a children's wear designer for a large clothing manufacturer in the U.S. She holds a B.S. degree from Auburn University in apparel design and textiles. She appeared on *Martha's Sewing Room* PBS television show for thirteen years as a regular guest and has taught classes at Martha Pullen's School of Art Fashion.

CHERYL R. DAVIDSON is the owner of A Frayed Knot heirloom sewing shop and the designer of Heirloom Originals in Lakeland, Tennessee. She teaches the art of fine hand sewing and construction in her shop and at many local businesses. She has served as an instructor at Martha Pullen's School of Art Fashion and is a primary designer and regular contributor to *Sew Beautiful* magazine. Visit her website at *www.heirloomoriginals.com*.

JANET GILBERT lives on a farm in Southern Illinois. She is an Air Force Veteran and holds a degree in Environmental Design from Texas A&M University and a Master's Degree from Troy State University. Janet is an active member of Smocking Arts Guild of America (SAGA). Janet is a regular contributor to *Sew Beautiful* magazine and has designed several original patterns for the publication. She and her husband have two adult sons and a 12-year-old daughter. Janet's daughter and new granddaughter are the inspiration behind her smocking designs and creative endeavors.

AMELIA JOHANSON has served as both editor and an associate editor for *Sew Beautiful* magazine for 24 years and in that capacity has contributed countless sewing articles to its pages. She also served as editor for many Martha Pullen publications as well as co-author for the *Kent State Museum* and *Victoria & Albert Museum* books. Prior to coming to Martha Pullen Company she was a fashion writer at the *Cleveland Plain Dealer* and *Columbus Dispatch* both in Ohio. She currently serves as a book acquisitions editor for F&W Media. She holds degrees in magazine journalism and home economics journalism from the University of Missouri in Columbia and lives in Medina, Ohio, with her husband and three sons.

HELEN LIVELY'S eclectic career path ranges from Plant Industrial Engineer in Manufacturing to Quality Assurance for a regional bank to Preschool Director to homeschool teacher to pattern designer and fiber artist. The thread through all has been her love of sewing and the challenge in studying classic techniques in order to use them in new ways. Her work has been published in previous issues of *Sew Beautiful* and SAGA News. Visit her website at *www.sewlively.com* for patterns, heirloom supplies, and one-of-a-kind handpainted silk fabrics.

CONNIE PALMER began sewing 25 years ago, and her gift for elegant design and exquisite craftsmanship has made her a highly sought-after teacher internationally. She has taught for numerous Martha Pullen events and can often be seen on MPTV, *America Sews with Sue Hausmann*, and *Quilting with Shar*. She is a regular contributor to *Sew Beautiful* magazine and works as a primary designer for Martha Pullen Company fulltime. Her work has also been featured on the cover of five Martha Pullen books.

SIVJE PARISH (pronounced SeeVee) lives in the California wine country, near the ocean and is a former interior decorator with the Laura Ashley Company. She has been sewing since she was five, but didn't received her first sewing machine until she was in high school, after winning the "Make It with Wool" competition. Both a pattern designer and tester, she loves to teach sewing and create custom dresses for her two daughters as well as for clients all over the world. Visit her blog at *goosegirlsews.blogspot.com* and find her patterns on *etsy.com/shop/sivjegoose*.

WENDY POCHE SCHOEN is an internationally known embroidery and pattern designer, educator, and author whose designs are regularly featured in *Sew Beautiful* magazine. Wendy has published five books on the subject of fine embroidery and sewing, over thirty patterns marketed under the name Petite Poche, and countless embroidery designs and kits. Her latest business venture includes the production of three hand embroidery DVDs, "Shadow Work Embroidery," "Basic Embroidery," and Embroidery II, and several machine embroidery disks, featuring Wendy's original embroidery designs in digital format. She is a well-known instructor of needle arts across the country and abroad. Her work has been published in *Sew Beautiful* magazine, *McCall's Needlework* magazine, *Creative Needle*, and *Inspirations* magazine. Wendy has hosted the hand-embroidery segments on *Martha's Sewing Room*, the public television show. She has completed the Royal School of Needlework Certificated program and is currently working toward a diploma.

SUE STEWART worked from 1990 to 2005 as a primary designer for Martha Pullen Company. During those years she authored dozens of featured articles in *Sew Beautiful* magazine, and for 8 years wrote "*Sue Says...*", a tips and tricks column. She also designed and sewed for *Martha's Sewing Room* and many Martha Pullen publications, and taught regularly at the SOAF. Since 2004 she has won several awards for her heirloom and machine-embroidered quilts, and has three quilts in the permanent collection of the National Quilt Museum. Visit her website at *www.SusanStewartDesigns.com* or contact her at *susanstewartdesigns@hotmail.com*.

LAURA JENKINS THOMPSON is well-known internationally in the sewing industry as a designer, author, and teacher. She has published numerous books, booklets, and designs for smocking, embroidery, and fine sewing by hand and machine. Since 1988, Laura has been a contributor to *Sew Beautiful*, *AS&E*, *Creative Needle*, and other fine needlework publications. She has studied embroidery in Paris and teaches a wide variety of classes in heirloom techniques. Laura also hosts her own bi-annual sewing retreat, *Stitchin' Charleston Style*, in historic Charleston, South Carolina. For more information, visit her website, *www.laurajenkinsthompson.com*.

MARIE YOLANDE is an international needlework instructor, author, and designer. She specializes in organizing needlework-themed tours to Europe that incorporate hands-on embroidery workshops with local skilled artisans. As her native language is French, many of the classes take place in France where there is a wealth of traditional needlework techniques. Yolande has written an English instructional book based on the boutis technique titled *Baby Layette à la Boutis Provençal*, which includes the entire pattern collection of a royal French layette. For information on her book, kits, workshops, and her needlework tour to the South of France to include Provence, Monaco, and the French Riviera, contact Marie at *marieyolande@att.net* or (770) 941-3102.

Resources

Aleene's® iLoveToCreate®
5673 E. Shields Ave.
Fresno, CA 93727
(800) 438-6226
www.ilovetocreate.com

Appleton Wool Thread
Alex-Baras Needlearts
1005 Hebron Ave.
Glastonbury, CT 06033
(860) 633-8503
store.apneedlearts.com

Baby Lock USA
www.babylock.com

Capitol Imports – Wholesale
PO Box 13022
Tallahasee, FL 32317
(850) 385-4665
capitolimports@talstar.com
www.laceimports.com

Clover Needlecraft, Inc
1441 S. Carlos Ave.
Ontario, CA 91761
(800) 233-1703
www.clover-usa.com

Coats & Clark
Consumer Services
PO Box 12229
Greenville, SC 29612
(800) 648-1479
www.coatsandclark.com

The DMC Corporation
10 Basin Dr., Ste. 130
Kearny, NJ 07032
(973) 589-0606
www.dmc-usa.com

Floriani
RNK Distributing
www.rnkdistributing.com
2562 Western Ave.
Knoxville, TN
(877) 331-0034

Helen Lively
Sew Lively Designs
Fort Smith, AR 72903
(479) 883-8942
www.sewlively.com
sewlively@me.com

Madeira USA LTD
30 Bayside Ct.
Laconia, NH 03246
(603) 528-2944
For United States Locations
(800) 225-3001
madeirausa.com

Isacord | Sewforless.com
American Sewing Machine
516 First Capitol Dr.
Saint Charles, MO 63301
(866) 739-2568
www.isacrodthread.com

Laura Jenkins Thompson
455 Rice Hope Dr.
Mt. Pleasant, SC 29464
www.laurajenkinsthompson.com

Marie Yolande
(770) 941-3102
marieyolande@att.net

Martha Pullen Company
149 Old Big Cove Rd.
Brownsboro, AL 35741
(256) 534-5200
store.marthapullen.com

Pellon® Consumer Products
(PCP Group LLC)
150 2nd Ave. N., Ste. 1400
St. Petersburg, FL 33701
(800) 223-5275
www.PellonProjects.com
www.Facebook.com/PellonProjects
www.Twitter.com/PellonProjects
www.pellonprojects.wordpress.com

Petite Poche (See Wendy Schoen)

Pilot Frixion
Pilot Corporation of America
3901 Regent Blvd.
Jacksonville, FL
(904) 645-9999
www.pilotpen.com

Robinson-Anton
PO Box 507
22 American St.
Mount Holly, NC 28120
Retail: (800) 847-3235
Wholesale: (800) 847-3236
www.robinson-anton.com

Soft Expressions Thread
1230 North Jefferson St., Ste. M
Anaheim, CA 92807
(714) 630-7414
(888) 545-8616
softexpressions.com

Southern Stitches Fine Sewing and
Custom-made Embroideries
Southern Stitches/Brer Rabbit Designs
website: *southern-stitches.com*
blog: *sewnso.blogspot.com*
twitter: *twitter.com/SewNso*

Sew Beautiful Magazine
Subscription Department
PO Box 421751
Palm Coast, FL 34142
(888) 825-5823
www.sewbeautifulmag.com

Wendy Poche Schoen
Retail shopping by appointment
2923 Tchoupitoulas St.
(Corner of 7th)
New Orleans, LA 70515
(504) 891-1025
www.wendyschoendesign.com

Sulky of America
980 Cobb Place Blvd., Ste. 130
Kennesaw, GA 30144
(800) 874-4115
www.sulky.com

Susan Bates
See Coats & Clark

Susan Stewart Designs
124 W. Monroe
Pittsburg, Kansas 66762
www.susanstewartdesigns.com

Wrights
Simplicity Creative Group
(800) 653-7301 ext. 4065
info@simplicity.com
www.simplicity.com/t-wrights.aspx

Zundt Design, Ltd - Wholesale
Denver, CO
(888) 533-7397
info@zundtdesign.com
www.zundtdesigns.com

Index